God's revelation for secular man, especially for secular man entering upon a reinvigorated, socially aware eschatological age.

In his final chapter, Heinrich Fries takes up the most direct challenge facing faith today — that of atheism. After careful consideration both of theoretical and practical atheism, and also of so-called Christian atheism and death-of-God theology, the author strives for a realization of faith as being not mere optimism for good in face of evil, but the witness of promise in time of trial.

In short, this book is filled not only with critique and answer, but with openness and a spirit of questioning. As a remarkable response of the author's own "faith under challenge," it becomes as well a challenge to be read with the same openness and spirit of questioning that are its distinctive traits.

This is perhaps the first truly comprehensive statement on Christian faith to be made since the beginning of the aggiornamento. In the finest tradition of popular scholarship, the renowned theologian Heinrich Fries here offers both a wide-ranging assessment of the pluralist milieu in which faith finds itself today, and an instructive guide on how faith must strengthen and improve itself if it is to survive and be useful to the here-and-now "Christian under challenge."

The author also controversially inquires into the recently emergent theology of hope, and concludes by allying hope to faith as its future dimension. This important theological argument has far-ranging consequences for the interpretation of

Faith under Challenge

Faith Under Challenge

Heinrich Fries

Translated by William D. Seidensticker

Herder and Herder

1969
HERDER AND HERDER NEW YORK
232 Madison Avenue, New York, N.Y. 10016

Original edition: *Herausgeforderter Glaube,*
Munich: Kösel-Verlag.

Nihil obstat: John M. T. Barton, s.t.d., l.s.s., Censor
Imprimatur: ✠ Patrick Casey, Vicar General
Westminster: 21 August 1969.

Library of Congress Catalog Card Number: 74-92317

Manufactured in the United States

Contents

Faith under Challenge

Preface

TODAY IT IS clear that the Christian faith is no longer something that can be taken for granted, but a question and a task—not only insofar as the individual must opt for this faith personally if it is to be and remain a living faith, but also insofar as this faith has become *questionable*, if we take that word in its most comprehensive meaning. That is to say, the Christian faith has been called in question, and at the same time it is worthy of being questioned. This status of inquiry, therefore, is by no means to be deplored or lamented in the name of faith. It would be a much more serious matter if faith were not, or no longer, questioned. In that case, it would have reached its end.

This inquiry into faith stems both from contemporary pluralism, whose world-views and ideologies are generally anti-Christian, and from science. Here the Christian faith is not only challenged, but is compelled to take up the challenge. If it were to refuse the challenge, or regard it as inadmissible or inappropriate, it would deny and reject itself. It would prove itself inauthentic and would no longer be questioned as a possibility. Faith, by its very nature, is a responding faith, and the believer must always be ready for, and capable of, this response. "Be ready always with an answer to everyone who asks a reason for the hope that is in you" (1 Peter 3: 15). Hope is a transcription of faith, its future dimension.

These remarks indicate the context in which the reflections in this book should be assessed and understood. It seeks to describe the fundamental traits of the Christian faith, and to determine the manner in which it is understood and grounded, the manner in which it is expressed and articulated, and the manner in which it puts itself critically in question (which is the very meaning of theology).

Consideration is given to some of the concrete challenges of the Christian faith, such as pluralism, secularism, and atheism.

An attempt will also be made to describe these phenomena and to come to grips with them on their own terms. We shall try to show that faith does not suppress these phenomena, but illuminates them. Our attention is also directed to the manner in which the Christian faith is itself to be understood when faced with this multiple challenge.

H. F.

CHAPTER ONE

The Christian Faith

THE REFLECTIONS offered in this book all have to do with the challenge against faith. But before the questions carried with this challenge can be dealt with individually, we must first consider faith itself. The faith we shall be dealing with is the Christian faith. The over-all problematic, "the challenge against faith," is particularly relevant to contemporary circumstances, in which the Christian faith is neither self-explanatory nor free from criticism, but is repeatedly called into question from a variety of viewpoints.

I

A brief glance at history is evidence enough of the uniqueness of the present age. The medieval period in Europe was characterized by a Christian faith within a Christian empire, where both "Church and world" were one. Even the massive and tragic (and to this day unreconciled) schism between the western and eastern Churches had not disturbed the essential unity of the Christian faith. To be sure, the Christian faith had its opposition, and even its antithesis, in the Middle Ages. Such counter-positions were presented by men and societies which were in no way unbelieving, but which believed in different things, and in a different manner, than did Christians; which proclaimed a message, other than the Christian one, and consequently attacked the Christian faith, specifically its *content*, the object of faith. Service to the faith, therefore, consisted in guaranteeing, expanding, and extending the matter of belief and the opportunity to believe it, over against those who accepted a different content of faith. The truth of the faith was more important than the freedom of the individual person. In case of conflict, the truth would certainly be chosen over freedom. But at that time the abiding and pervading feature of faith was its specification as a human act and perfection. The medievals knew and lived the fact that faith belongs to man because man is *the* one being who can believe, who, without faith, cannot live and exist humanly. Moreover, their faith cut through all differences and was directed expressly to God. It was belief in God, religious belief, a faith that recognized and worshipped God as the obscure personal power reigning absolutely over man and his world. That is all the more striking when we consider that at that time the Christian faith was articulated above all in opposition to the Jews and Mohammedans, who believed not only in God, but in the God revealed in history, who spoke through Moses and the prophets, who was involved in the history of the people of Israel. The question of faith was thus narrowed and focussed on the question, "What do you think of the Christ?" (Matthew 22: 42). That is what divided, and still divides, the minds of Christians, Jews, and Mohammedans. But it is important to note that differences with regard to the content, object, and truth of faith were encompassed by the common fact of faith as such, as well as belief in God, and further, in the God who has communicated himself in word and in history.

Today, on the other hand, there is an entirely different situation. The Christian faith is opposed in a number of ways. Some of these we shall discuss later on, but one is obvious and ought to be mentioned now. It is a mode of opposition that does not at all fit into the common religious milieu that was characteristic of the Middle Ages. Today *everything* is brought into question. Not only are the tenets of faith argued and debated, but faith itself is challenged as being a relic of man's primitive state.

Further, especially after the division of western Christianity, questions of faith were often viewed as an internal affair—brought about by the numerous and various attitudes towards faith of the different confessions. What is new in our day is the fact that beyond what is unique to each confession or church, a common consideration of the Christian faith seems to be something not only possible and significant, but imperative. One reason for this situation is that modern opposition to faith is generally not discriminative of confessional peculiarities but rejects faith as such. It should be mentioned at this point that this opposition is not only or necessarily aggressive; it can also take the form of simple but absolute disinterest. Thus the various confessions have been brought together for a number of reasons into a bond of mutuality that in a sense transcends their differences. This we shall discuss later at some length.

In sum: the Christian faith today is no longer as self-contained as it was in the Middle Ages, but at the same time it is not as divided and quarrelsome as it was in the so-called confessional period and in the pre-Council era. Any consideration of the Christian faith must be set off against this background.

II

Deeper reflection on the Christian faith rests on a distinction that is basic in theology—the science of faith. Faith may be regarded both as the *act* of faith, that is, the act and activity of the believing man: *fides qua creditur*; and as the *object*, content, and truth of faith, that is, that which is to be believed and accepted in faith: *fides quae creditur.*

Today it is necessary to speak of the Christian faith primarily in the sense of the act and activity of faith. This assertion reintroduces an earlier distinction, and in a twofold manner. When men spoke of faith in the Middle Ages, they presupposed the act and activity of faith as obvious and given. Faith, for them, was essentially the content and truth of faith. Protection of the faith meant protection of the truth of faith, not protection of the free decision to believe for everyone, but specifically for the Christian, the "orthodox" believer.

At the time of the Reformation, act and object became traits of belief. Protestants tended to emphasize the act of faith as an act of surrender and trust, as submission to God (without thereby altogether ignoring content—a fact attested to by the appearance of different denominations, each with its own unique literature). The Catholic viewpoint, without wholly ignoring the act of faith, placed greater stress on the content and articles of faith. Thus it emphasized the intellectual and rational element of faith, and accentuated the role of the *church*, particularly the teaching church. As it stands in the catechism, faith means: "to hold as true what God has revealed and puts forth through his Church for belief." This approach regards it as important that nothing that has been revealed and put forth by the Church should be omitted, because the contents of faith are related to each other, and are so essentially connected that they form a systematic whole from which no part can be removed.

In terms of the Protestant approach, faith was considered to be a personal encounter, and the truth of this faith was "truth as encounter." From the Catholic point of view, faith was the belief that something is true (as it was readily characterized by the Protestants)—an impersonal relation to truths, to what is objectively given. Moreover, faith was considered to be the "work of mankind," which had to be carried out and perfected for salvation.[1]

Thus, as a consequence, what in themselves were meaningful distinctions and accentuations in the understanding of faith became the marks of different denominations and produced a schism. That was separated which God had joined together. Today we are in a position to recognize biases that threaten to calcify, and to work for a greater unity in which all the elements of faith fit together.

When we take a look at the contemporary situation and realize that not only particular contents of faith pose difficulties for contemporary man (including the contemporary Christian), but the Christian faith in itself as such (*above all* its dogmatic statements), both as act and possibility, then it becomes imperative to take up the matter of "the Christian faith" beginning with a consideration of these fundamental points.[2]

[1] Cf. H. Fries, *Revelation* (New York, 1968), *passim.*

[2] Several studies from the sparse literature on this topic can be recommended: M. Seckler, "Glaube," in *Handbuch theol. Grundbegriffe* I

The Christian faith obviously is a matter of belief. That is no tautology. What it means is that the Christian faith pertains to the attitude or state which we call belief, which is found in human experience primarily in the form: "I believe in you," or "I believe you." Even in this common form, belief is a personal act, an engagement with the "Thou" of another person, a confrontation and acquaintance with him, a participation in his being, life, thought, attitudes, dispositions, desires, and loves. Without belief, human experience would be utterly unthinkable and incomplete.[3]

According to the testimony of the Bible, belief in God stands squarely in this dimension of personal interaction. This testimony can be illustrated with an example. The father of the believer, of all believers, and therefore of the Christian believer, is Abraham. In him, his life, his fate, his conduct, like an exemplary model, it becomes clear what belief is, namely, to turn oneself unconditionally to God, whose word and command Abraham made known, for example in the call and promise, "Leave your country, your kinsfolk, and your father's house, for the land which I will show you; I will make a great nation of you" (Genesis 12: 1f.); and in the order, "Take your only son Isaac whom you love . . . and offer him as a holocaust . . ." (Genesis 22: 2). Abraham believes, and that means that he presents himself and his entire life to God, who makes known to him to do so. He obeys and remains true to this obedience even though (and this is also a part of belief) all experience, all human insight and expectation speak against it. This word of God, however, means more to him than any other. It is that which he attends to and after which he follows. It is the energy that helps him go his way into the unknown, into the implausible, into the paradoxical, into the seemingly impossible and unexpected. It is

---

(Munich, 1962), pp. 528–548; J. Trütsch and J. Pfammatter, "Der Glaube," in *Mysterium Salutis* (Einsiedeln–Zürich–Cologne, 1963), pp. 791–903.

[3] Cf. J. Mouroux, *I Believe* (London and New York, 1959); A. Brunner, *Glaube und Erkenntnis* (Munich, 1951); H. Fries, *Glauben—Wissen* (Berlin, 1960); J. Pieper, *Über den Glauben*. ET *Belief and Faith* (New York, 1963).

clear in Abraham's character—belief signifies presence in, being grounded in, God, his word, his will; it signifies total involvement in God and his mystery. As is clear in the Hebrew word for "believe," belief means to say yes and amen. Amen—so it is; amen—so it may be. On this basis, to believe, in the Old Testament, means the same as to live in God. The high point of this state of being for the people who live in faith, who exist in it concretely and historically, is expressed in the familiar passage from Isaiah (7: 9): "If you will not believe, you shall not continue."[4]

This example makes it clear that belief signifies a comprehensive claim on the whole man, and that such a claim is possible in completeness only with respect to God. Thus only a partial, deficient form of belief enters into faith as an intra-human attitude. *The whole man, God alone*—that is the true, fundamental situation of belief.

As a consequence it is clear that faith signifies an activity, a radical act of self-surrender, as well as including in itself the assent to specific matters, claims, disclosures, and promises. Without this assent, faith does not attain its complete form and realization. The essential relationship is to be conceived in such a way that the assent to all concrete matters of faith is grounded in the fact that the believer turns himself completely, totally, and unconditionally to God as God communicates and reveals himself. All forms of "I believe that..." are grounded in the form "I believe in you." Otherwise the earnestness of the act of faith, as the surrender of man to the absolute Thou of the mysterious God—the whole man, God alone—would be tried and tested by the fact that man is involved in what is concrete, namely, in the explicit word, the concrete command, the special promise, which, for the most part, are contrary to all human designs, expectations, ideas, and possibilities.

The *Christian faith* also draws itself in line with the exemplary belief lived by and represented in Abraham. Abraham is the "father of us all" in faith (Romans 4: 16); and in faith, as Paul

[4] Cf. A. Weiser and R. Bultmann, "πιστεύω," in *Theol. Wörterbuch zum Neuen Testament* V (Stuttgart, 1959), pp. 174–230.

and John say (Romans 4: 11f.; Galatians 3: 6f.; John 8: 39), we are his true sons. Our Christian faith signifies the surrender of our whole self to *the* God who spoke to Abraham and his people, who involved himself in their history, and who spoke his final, complete, and unsurpassable Word in Jesus Christ (see Hebrews 1: 1)—in Jesus, who not only proclaimed God's message, but who is himself the content of this message in the mystery of his person, in the claim of his word, and in the deed of his work. In Jesus Christ and his life it has been revealed who God is, how he is disposed, and what his intentions are for mankind. The Christian faith believes that, as it is said in John's Gospel, Jesus is the absolute "I am he" (8: 24; 13: 19), the pure Revealer in an exclusive, absolute sense: "No one has at any time seen God. The only begotten Son, who is in the bosom of the Father, he has revealed him" (1: 18). Therefore, Jesus, according to John's account, claims, "He who sees me sees also the Father" (14: 9).

The Christian faith believes in the God who became flesh in Jesus of Nazareth and took on the human condition, who raised this Jesus, who had been crucified, from the dead, and made him Savior, Redeemer, Reconciler, Lord, and the Anointed. According to another version, the Christian faith believes in Jesus Christ in whom God finally spoke and acted. It believes in the person of Jesus Christ, in the Christ event, in which the reconciliation, redemption, and salvation of the world were accomplished, in which the glory of God has appeared, and in which the invitation and offer of the love of God remains open until the end of the world.

To believe in Christ means to be grounded and to exist in Jesus Christ, as expressed in the passage from Paul: "It is now no longer I that live, but Christ lives in me" (Galatians 2: 20). Faith, therefore, is a way in which Christ lives in us (Ephesians 3: 17). The Christian faith signifies participation in Jesus, "who, having risen from the dead, dies no longer" (Romans 8: 9). It means to be disposed as he was disposed (Philippians 2: 5), to undertake the way of Jesus into the true way of life.

Consequently, the Christian faith is principally and primarily a *personal* relationship. The Christian believes in the God who spoke his final Word in Christ. He believes in Jesus Christ, who is his Lord and Redeemer, the ground of his salvation, and the hope of his life and death.

This radically personal Christian faith, however, at the same time articulates a content. It is for this reason that the Christian faith can be so characterized by Paul: I believe that Jesus is the Christ and the Kyrios, the Lord (Romans 10: 9). As the Christ, he is the fulfillment of all the Old Testament statements and promises that pertain to the Advent and to the One who is to come. As Paul declared in his Second Epistle to the Corinthians, in Jesus Christ the "Yes" has come. "For all the promises of God find their 'Yes' in him; and therefore through him also rises the 'Amen' to God unto our glory" (1: 20). As the Lord, the Kyrios, Jesus Christ is *he* whom God has raised from the dead and made into the Lord of the living and the dead.[5] These statements about Jesus Christ articulate the personal belief in Christ and sketch out its dimensions, while all statements that express a content are encompassed by the fundamental "I believe in you."

In the Christian faith, act, activity, and content are intimately connected with each other and directly condition each other. Without concrete content the Christian faith is empty; without a personal reference and relatedness, it is blind, impersonal, and dead. No element can dispense with the others. If one is played off against another, the whole is at stake. However, if it should be asked where the critical starting point is to be located, the answer must be: in belief in the sense of being grounded and present in Jesus Christ. Whoever has done this to perfection will be given everything else besides. He will have the power of assenting to the content of concrete statements. Thus the Christian faith is not a specific task, but a way of living.

Because Jesus Christ is the absolute fulfillment of the self-communication of God, and at the same time the absolute fulfillment of what faith most radically means (namely, that

[5] Cf. O. Kuss, "Der Glaube nach den paulinischen Hauptbriefen," in *Auslegung und Verkündigung* I (Regensburg, 1963), pp. 187–212.

Jesus is "the author and finisher of faith" [Hebrews 12: 2]), the faith that believes this is the fulfillment of faith. Thus it is not at all paradoxical or misguided, but rather eminently meaningful and legitimate, to speak of the Christian as the pure believer. That means that all the elements constituting belief in God, as found in all true religions, but especially as they were realized in the faith of the people of Israel, are integrated into the Christian faith. Looked at from the other side, it means that faith, as the conduct of man with regard to God and as the engagement of man with him, cannot ultimately be perfected without the fulfillment present in the Christian faith. That holds at the very level of the given, of possibilities and conditions. (It does not exclude the possibility that a non-Christian might personally attain belief in God more intensively and existentially than one who acknowledges the Christian faith verbally or externally, but does not bring it to realization.)

Consequently, the Christian faith is the most complete form of faith as such, and of belief in God, or religious faith, in particular. Even today, it is the guarantee of both kinds of faith. It is their advocate and representative.

III

If the Christian faith is the total surrender of the whole man to God alone, who came to us in Jesus Christ, his son, who spoke with us and lived with us, then it follows that what appears in the act and activity of faith and in the acceptance of its content intimately confronts and concerns the believer. It means that it should not be merely a matter of knowledge, but should take in the man. His life is defined to the extent that he lives in such a faith, that faith becomes active, that, biblically speaking, he "bears fruit."

Faith signifies the daily turning away from the danger and temptation to refuse faith and its word, and therewith God—to close ourselves in ourselves in a mistaken autonomy, anthropocentrism, and worldliness. Faith means to beg each day, "Lord, I believe; help my unbelief" (Mark 9: 24), for in the believer belief and unbelief run together. Faith means to imitate Jesus Christ, to be ready to assume his fate: the cross and resurrection. Belief means to have the mind and spirit of Jesus Christ (see 1 Corinthians 2: 16), to mold one's life and all that it contains in such a way that faith becomes the light that enlightens the believer, that illuminates the ways of existence, that frees the energies and vital forces that our life requires each day.

The light and life that stem from faith, however, in no way alienate man, or falsify his life, or remove him from his immediate tasks and necessities. That is the criticism of Marxism, which regards Christian faith as an ideology. Faith is not something forced upon mankind, a burden to it. Rather, in faith man freely determines himself and what is truly his—his character, his origins, his future, and the meaning of his life. Faith signifies and establishes the fact that, as Bultmann has said, "man is freed from himself for himself,"[6] and that he accepts the humanity that is grounded in and owes everything to God, and the human and social questions that this humanity entails: tolerance, freedom, love, hope, the overcoming of fear and doubt, and so forth.

This approach should in no way be taken to mean that the Christian faith exhausts itself in the illumination and realization of existence, that is, as a means to an end. It is rather the case that whoever believes, totally and unconditionally, attains a true understanding and realization of what it means to be human in the act of surrender and in the readiness to receive the message of faith. He knows then and realizes that the content contained in and communicated by faith, such as that found in the confessions of faith and in dogma, are not arbitrarily imposed restrictions or the pronouncement of strange, alien, and improbable facts that have no connection whatsoever to the concrete life and existence of mankind, but rather that they are "truths for me" and that they answer the questions of the human mind and heart. The question that includes both the openness and demand for inquiry and defines the scope and limits of

[6] "Neues Testament und Mythologie," in *Kerygma und Mythos* I, edited by H. W. Bartsch (Hamburg[2], 1951), p. 39.

humanity, is an "urphenomenon" of mankind. As an inquirer and a hearer, as one in need of salvation, man is related to everything that is expressed in faith. On the other hand, it must be added as a clarification and a specification that the truths and contents of the Christian faith are significant in themselves as the revelation of the wisdom, lordship, and love of God. They do not derive their truth and legitimacy from anthropological components. That is not to deny, however, that the content of faith has an anthropological dimension. Indeed, its content attests to the works of God, who has disclosed himself and acted "for mankind and for the sake of our salvation." It is in this way that theology is theological anthropology. Such an approach is not at all opposed to the necessary theocentrism of the whole of theology, but it does stand "in opposition to the opinion that man is only one theme among others in theology, or that we can speak about God theologically without saying something about man, and vice versa."[7]

IV

In describing that dimension of the Christian faith that relates to man, it becomes clear that the Christian faith is thoroughly related to past events in history, that is, to what happened "at that time" and what has been reported about it. In distinction from all historical events that are *merely* historical, however, the past attested to by the Christian faith is at the same time always *present*. It endures, and will do so until the end of the world. For the revelation perfected in Jesus Christ happened once, and at the same time for all time. It is the final, complete, and therefore enduring Word of God. It is the self-communication of God that is unsurpassable in history, lastingly effective in history, the ground of history, the vanquisher of sin and death.[8] Thus the Christian faith has its support in history, but at the same time it lives in the present and is held in suspension by the future and

[7] K. Rahner, "Theologie und Anthropologie," in *Wahrheit und Verkündigung* II, edited by L. Scheffczyk, W. Dettloff, and R. Heinzmann (Munich–Paderborn–Vienna, 1967), p. 1389.

[8] Cf. *Dogmatic Constitution on Divine Revelation* I, 4.

the hope it contains. The future and hope, however, are the gift and the dimension of faith itself. The basis for this conclusion is the fact that Jesus, who came and died on the cross, is also the exalted and living Christ, who dies no more and who establishes an everlasting present and presence in the transcendence of his resurrection from the dead and in the Spirit that he has sent. This presence of Jesus Christ is found in many ways: in word, in the sacraments, in the liturgy, in faith, in the community of the Church (whose head and life he is), in mankind, in our "neighbor," in the "least" of our brethren (with whom Christ identifies himself in a very special way—see Matthew 25: 35–40, 42–45). Consequently, Jesus Christ is contemporaneous with our faith and the faith of any time.

It follows directly that the Christian faith cannot be satisfied with merely reiterating its content without regard to time or place. Faith, for its own sake, strives for an ever deeper and more personal appropriation of what is believed. This appropriation depends in particular on understanding—the penetration of the mind into the interconnections of the contents of faith. This understanding places the content of what is believed in new and different perspectives which are in no way additions to what is essential, but are its deeper manifestation. Thus there is growth in faith through seeing it proceed from a single light and converge back into it again. It leads to the articles of the confession of faith and the articulation of dogma, for example the mystery of the person of Jesus Christ as contained in the word "God-man" and in the formula "one person in two natures." Such terminology is not ordinarily found in the Bible, but these different categories attempt to give formulation to what is said there—but in different words and images, in a different language, and against a different horizon of understanding.

We are then faced with a situation that has brought so many problems to light today: that, because the Christian faith is and should be *our* faith today, faith must be contemporary as well as personal. The content of faith must so be translated as to meet changing situations in such a way that the content remains intact while at the same time reaching contemporary man in his specific historical situation, according to the circumstances of his way of understanding and his world-view, so that it can be accepted by him as *his* Christian faith freely, sincerely, and convincingly. There can be advantages, therefore, in using words other than those of the Bible in order to say *what* the Bible means. This holds with even greater force for various formulations of the content of faith throughout the history of faith and dogma by means of specific philosophical categories. This reservation touches on the important distinction between the content and the form of faith, between facts and the structure of language, between the truth and the history of faith. To attend to this reservation and to draw its consequences is by no means a betrayal and surrender of faith. It is rather what is expected of a living faith, the Christian faith today.

There is a further consideration. If the Christian faith is living and has an immediate relation to the present, as we have discussed the matter, and if every age has its own questions and its own need for answers, then this faith must be seen as posed in terms of such questions. Consequently, it cannot merely repeat formulas and vocabularies of yesterday. It must inject them into the contemporary horizon of inquiry and formulate the statements of faith as answers to today's, not yesterday's, questions, without uprooting the content of faith. Sometimes it is sufficient if new aspects of faith come into view, or if new words are introduced into the language.

It should be fairly clear from the above that the Christian faith today as such is not properly called into question. We have said too that the Christian faith today must supply answers that are common to all the Christian denominations. Such a situation not only makes possible but promotes a common effort, a truly ecumenical cooperation towards truth. Of course, we must yet add that the Christian faith cannot supply an unequivocal answer for all questions, and that in some cases several answers are possible. If the Christian faith were an answer for all questions, it would no longer be faith, and the God in whom we believe would no longer be the free, ordaining, and sovereign

Lord, but the God who, according to Ludwig Feuerbach, was created in man's own image.

V

We come now to a further point: that the Christian faith is something *secondary* to the primary and preceding initiative of God, who gives himself to men in grace and reveals to them their salvation. The Christian faith is the *answer* to the word of God, the response to divine action, the reception of the gift that is meant for us but which is not ours to give.

Faith is something secondary as distinct from what is primary, which God brings about and reveals. However, man's faith response is not something unilaterally spontaneous, but the gift of God to man, which he accepts thankfully and which he is thankfully permitted to make his own insofar as he says: I believe.

That men recognize the guidance and predestination of God in the history of Israel; that they see in Jesus of Nazareth not merely "the son of a carpenter" (see Matthew 13: 55), but the incarnate *Logos* and revealer of the glory of God; that they see in the cross of Christ not the tragic fate and despairing end of a god-forsaken man, or scandal and folly (see 1 Corinthians 1: 23), but the sign of salvation and the act of reconciliation; that they realize that the greatest humiliation is the highest revelation of God; that men are not scandalized at the ways and manners of God, but recognize in them the hidden workings of God guided by love—all of this is not the fruit of human insight. "Flesh and blood have not revealed this" to mankind (see Matthew 16: 17), for then it would have been proposed and would have functioned quite differently. It was presented, revealed, disclosed, given in the light of faith, in the eyes of faith, in the grace of faith.

The wonderful words of the Reformation—faith alone, grace alone, Christ alone, the word alone—have their full Christian significance in this regard, a meaning intended for all Christians.

What man can do in this process is to be open, to be ready to receive, to hear, to reform.

A sign and indication that faith is a gift, an endowment, grace, something received, is the fact that it is communicated through the *Church.* The individual believes, and is believing, insofar as he is accepted into the community of believers, or, as the Bible says, is "added" to this community (see Acts 2: 41). This is the meaning of the question asked at the administration of baptism: "What do you desire of the Church?" and the answer: "Faith." The Christian faith cannot be produced subjectively from within a man. He must accept it and receive it from those who have received it, from the community of believers, in which the faith of the first witnesses, and the testimony of those who first believed, the faith and testimony of the apostles and prophets, lives and remains a presence.

These connections clarify the meaning and the function of the Church for faith: it assumes the service of the faith through preaching, witness, teaching, word, and sacraments.

VI

We have so far attempted to present a few thoughts on the transdimensional theme of the Christian faith in general, with specific reference to the contemporary intellectual climate. If we now return to the point at which we initiated these considerations, we can see that the Christian faith today is set off against a viewpoint that seeks to eliminate all forms and influences of faith by opting not for faith, but for criticism and scepticism, or for exact science exclusively, in the form of logically evident demonstration, mathematical calculation, or the causal explanation of empirical facts. Adherents to this viewpoint fail to realize that in the exercise of such an option science itself operates at the level of world-view, faith, religion, a situation which Karl Jaspers has labelled "scientific superstition."[9] For such a claim goes far beyond what science as such can bring about (and, if it remains true to its methods, would want to bring about). Whoever rejects faith as a fundamental option of mankind fails to take into account some very important areas of life, particularly those areas that have to do

[9] K. Jaspers and R. Bultmann, *Die Frage der Entmythologisierung* (Munich, 1954), p. 11. ET *Myth and Christianity* (New York, 1958).

with the person and those human dimensions that we call freedom, or love, transcendence. Christian faith is set off from that attitude which denies faith in all forms. It stands as representative of the dignity of faith as such.

Christian faith—the act of faith and assent to the content of faith—is also to be distinguished from that kind of faith which regards belief as fundamentally a personal act, but something uncertain because it is necessary for faith to avoid any sort of articulation of what is believed. It follows the axiom: what is important is simply *that* you believe; it is not important *what* you believe. Christian faith, on the contrary, while agreeing that the "thatness" of faith is essential, insists also that this aspect has its base and support in the content of faith—in that which you believe, and especially in that in which you believe. The Christian faith describes this content in its articulated confession of faith. It does not believe in an anonymous transcendence, or in a divinity that is alienated from the world, but in the God who has entered into time and the world, who took on human form in Jesus Christ and endured the human condition until his death on the cross. The Christian faith, through its acknowledgement of this God, is the advocate of every religious faith, every belief in God, and acts as their representative. Thus it is a service for all mankind.

Finally, contrary to any purely subjective or enthusiastic approach to the Christian faith, which denies the Church and all forms of ecclesiasticism and seeks radical immediacy, we understand the Christian faith as one for which we are indebted to the Church and to the community of believers, and which we live in this community, in which we recognize the institution of him whom we believe—who, for the sake of faith, gave mission, structure, and form to the Church, which is the very content and mystery of faith. This statement does not exclude, but rather includes, the fact that the Church can often make faith difficult, and often poses the most difficult problem for faith.

The situations which the Christian faith confronts today constitute a unique threat. It is a fortunate blessing that at the same time we have learned to view faith in its totality and in the realization of all of its accents and dimensions. It is also fortunate that we have learned anew to see the community within the Christian faith.

A further blessing and task can be seen in these things if we realize (and this recognition requires the sincerity that we owe to our Christian faith) that today we have not merely one tradition of the Christian faith to preserve, nor can we represent faith merely in the form of tradition; rather, with due respect for tradition (without which we would collapse for want of a foundation), we have to live and actualize Christian faith as a personal decision—as the irreplaceable "*I believe.*"

CHAPTER TWO

Is Faith Defenseless?

OUR CONCERN in this chapter will be to inquire into a question that is not only contemporary but one that is asked with some frequency and insistence, namely, whether faith, especially Christian faith, is defenseless. Our treatment should not be understood in a moralistic, pedagogical, psychological, or sociological sense (although today we find many problems and difficulties here), but insofar as the intellectual or rational foundations of faith appear to be very unsteady. Faith shows itself to be defenseless insofar as it is incapable of giving an adequate account of its premisses and contents, either to itself or to others; that is, insofar as it is not firm, confident, free, and open, but seems to be defeated and overrun by questions posed today in the name of knowledge or science, or in the name of thorough and radical criticism.

One approach to Christian faith might see a special characteristic, even an advantage, in its defenselessness and defeat. This approach holds that faith is bound, the testimony of which is the cross, a scandal and folly when viewed through the eyes of the world (1 Corinthians 1: 23). Every attempt to defend the faith is a betrayal, an impudently human, unbelieving demand for certainty, an unallowable bid for control. To be defenseless is precisely the glory of faith. Thus Rudolf Bultmann has written, "Man, who wants to believe in God as his God, must realize that he possesses nothing on the basis of which he could believe, that he is, as it were, suspended in mid-air and can demand no proof for the truth of the word that is spoken to him. Only he finds certainty who lets all certainty go, who, as Luther put it, is ready to enter into the inner darkness."[1]

[1] *Kerygma und Mythos* II, edited by H. W. Bartsch (Hamburg, 1952), p. 207.

Here the "defenselessness of faith" is neither a question nor a concern, but a theological thesis.

From the Catholic point of view, this conception of the Christian faith, of *sola fides* conceived in this way, for all its seriousness and impressive grandeur is too radical and one-sided. One might almost say that it is trans-human. In the Catholic understanding of the phrase, "the defenselessness of faith" is not a self-evident or self-sufficient thesis but a real question concerning the credibility of faith, and beyond that a concern for faith and for the believing man.

The defenselessness of faith mainly concerns its *questionability in terms of knowledge*. We are thus face to face with the question of the mutual relations between knowledge and faith.[2] Defenseless faith, as a question, simply demands an application of such a relationship. This theme, furthermore, is given with the very matter of faith.

Ever since the beginning of the modern times, and today still, it is common to find the relationship between knowledge and faith reduced to the formula: faith means as much as not to know at all, or to know only provisionally, half-way, or superficially. Not only is a distinction made between the two realms, but it is made in such a way as to detract from faith's ability to apprehend what is true. If knowledge is taken to mean a mode of cognition that is grounded, guaranteed, and capable of exact verification; if cognition signifies an intellectual appropriation of what is; and if the grounding and certainty of cognition depend on actual insight and experience, then it would appear that faith is hopelessly inferior to knowledge. Faith thus clearly means the renunciation of actual experience and insight and the acceptance of statements and points of view on the basis of authority and the testimony of others. Faith is all the more itself, and is praised all the more, when it does not want to see (John 20: 29), but is rather a blind faith. Finally, the reality that is given in faith—in belief in God and in Christian faith—is the realm of what cannot be seen (see Hebrews 11: 1), of

[2] Cf. A. Brunner, *Glaube und Erkenntnis* (Munich, 1951); H. Fries, *Glauben—Wissen* (Berlin, 1960); H. Urs von Balthasar, *Herrlichkeit: Eine theologische Ästhetik* I: *Schau der Gestalt* (Einsiedeln, 1961).

the inaccessible and uncontrollable, which borders the unreal. Thus the man who both believes and knows must adopt a double standard in the assignment of truth, or in similar fashion, must separate faith and knowledge in terms of act and object, in such a way that no bridges lead from one to the other. But even then the defenselessness of faith is manifest. For this view attempts to elevate the provisional and inferior knowledge offered by faith to the grounded insight of scientific knowledge, and to unmask and reject as unscientific, rhetorical, or ideological all statements and claims of faith that do not conform to this standard. Several points of view may be developed with regard to this thematic situation.

I

It is of note that in the Bible, especially in the New Testament, there is no mention of any opposition between faith and sure knowledge. On the contrary, as a reading of John's Gospel will show, faith and knowledge are one. Both concepts are used interchangeably and one can replace for the other. Faith and knowledge form a living whole and unity. Knowledge is an intensive form of faith, and faith is the source of knowledge.[3]

In early Christian times, those who came to the faith from philosophy understood this faith as true philosophy (Justin), or, along with Clement and Origen of Alexandria, as the essence of knowledge (*gnosis*). The theological thought of the Middle Ages expressed the proximity and inner relationship of faith and knowledge in the well-known axioms, "I believe, that I might know (understand)," and "I know, that I might believe." Thomas of Aquin, who was deeply aware of the distinction between faith and knowledge, drew together in his *Summa* the various ways and orders of faith and knowledge in the unity and totality of truth (that is, truth cannot contradict truth), and grounded truth in God, the source and goal of faith and knowledge. Faith, here,

[3] H. Schlier, "Glauben, Erkennen, Lieben nach dem Johannesevangelium," in *Einsicht und Glaube*, edited by J. Ratzinger and H. Fries (Freiburg–Basel–Vienna, 1962), pp. 98–111; R. Bultmann, *Theology of the New Testament* I–II (New York, 1951, 1955); R. Schnackenburg, *The Gospel According to St. John* I (London and New York, 1968).

was not defenseless; rather, we find a defense grounded in the harmony of faith and knowledge.

Towards the end of the Middle Ages and the beginning of modern times, this image of order and unity began to break down; tragic and serious conflicts soon broke out between theologians and exponents of the newly founded natural sciences, with the result that a barrier of mutual antagonism was established. Friedrich Dessauer regards these mutual attacks (that is, of faith in the name of knowledge and knowledge in the name of faith, and the mutual losses that ensued) as one of the major catastrophes of the Western world, one that can be compared only with the major schisms in Christianity.[4] This situation was intensified and decisively deepened by modern philosophy and its orientation in autonomous reason. Such a division is all the more tragic in that it was not necessary, since there is a theological, Christian anthropocentrism grounded in faith.[5] The gulf became all the wider when (since thought and science, in the strict sense, were considered possible only for the realms of experience, mathematics, and the natural sciences) the "reliable results" of natural science (and later, history) were pitted against the statements of faith and revelation. The critical philosophy of Kant (who wanted to restrict knowledge "in order to make room for faith") gave explicit articulation to the dualism between faith and knowledge in a manner that has been extremely influential. Critical philosophy has brought particular attention to the defenselessness of faith. It is also expressed in the admission of Friedrich Heinrich Jacobi that he desired to be "a pagan in mind, and a Christian in feeling." German Idealism, on the other hand, above all in Hegel, attempted a complete, speculative penetration of the Christian faith in order to "draw it up" (in the several meanings of *aufheben*) into the conceptual form of thought and knowledge. Here faith was indeed no longer defenseless, but it had become so shackled with armor as to become a cripple.

[4] F. Dessauer, *Der Fall Galilei und wir* (Frankfurt, 1957).

[5] Cf. J. B. Metz, *Christian Anthropology* (New York, 1968); K. Rahner, "Theologie und Anthropologie," in *Wahrheit und Verkündigung* II, pp. 1389–1407.

The separation, or at least the dualism, of faith and knowledge in the course of the nineteenth century was particularly preserved wherever it was stipulated that knowledge is possible only in the realm of mathematics and natural science, or wherever natural science was expanded into a world-view that claimed competence in all questions. This situation was likely to be intensified if, for example, a school of philosophy made a similar universal claim, or, to take a specific example, when Christian faith was directly attacked by the so-called "second Enlightenment" as being mythically structured ideology.[6]

Recently the more influential figures of science have repudiated such universality for their discipline, and speak of a scientific theory of the world with very precise limits since they wish to consider only that part of reality that is accessible to their instruments and methods. Beyond these limits, the knowledge of science leaves open (and even seeks) an answer that it cannot itself give, but must receive from beyond its limits as relevant to its questions and answers: with regard, for example, to the meaning of life and human responsibility in face of the possibilities and dangers raised by natural science and technology.

Of course, answers to such questions are denied the character of true knowledge. They are referred to the realm of faith, as distinct from scientific (that is, empirico-positivistic) knowledge, or to the realm of metaphysics and philosophy, which are not well thought of since they are "unscientific."

Contemporary philosophy, on the other hand, especially existentialism and personalism, bring clear awareness to the meaning of faith as a fundamental determination of man. This represents a great liberation, restoring dignity and value to faith as a fundamental human phenomenon. However, even here, the Christian faith finds itself under attack: on the one hand by the Old Testament faith (Martin Buber),[7] and above all by "philosophical faith" (Karl Jaspers),[8] which set up a dualism of incompatibility and thus

[6] Cf. G. Szczesny, *Die Zukunft des Unglaubens* (Munich, 1958).

[7] M. Buber, *Two Types of Faith* (London and New York, 1961).

[8] K. Jaspers, *Philosophy and the World* (Chicago, 1963); and *Philosophical Faith and Revelation* (New York, 1967); cf. H. Fries, *Ärgernis und Widerspruch* (Würzburg, 1965), pp. 41–99.

a new sort of defenselessness of faith, because both are concerned with the ground and the totality of existence.[9]

II

In order to gain clarity in the question of the defenselessness of faith, it is necessary to develop a genuine idea of faith itself. The fundamental structure of faith takes on the form, "I believe in you," "I believe you," as we saw in the first chapter. "I believe in you" is of a higher order than "I believe you." It is total and comprehensive and engages mankind in a radical manner.[10] The statement "I believe something" is not the fundamental but the secondary form of belief. It conceals the nature of faith and leads easily to the view that faith is identical with mere conjecture or arbitrary opinion. We can conclude that faith, fundamentally and essentially, is not a relation of man to things, statements, or formulas, but signifies a relation to *persons*. The latin *credere* comes from *cor dare* (to give one's heart), and gives striking expression to the personal structure of faith. The relation of faith to the person above all else has to do with *knowledge* of the person. Faith is the mode and manner in which we gain access to knowledge of the person. The truth of this conclusion is so strong that without faith the depths and nature of the reality and mystery of the person remain closed. The problem of the defenselessness of faith thereby moves into a new light. For the (apparently unbridgeable) dualism between faith and knowledge or thought, and the resulting defenselessness of faith, is thus shattered.

The true nature of the person cannot be known by subjecting it to analysis through experimentation and testing, or by describing it as the sum of sociological, economic, biological, and psychical factors. No matter how important, instructive, and indispensable such knowledge may be, it will not lead us to what is ultimately important, namely, the true, inner nature of the person. A knowledge of the person according to the accepted methods of logic,

[9] Cf. H. Gollwitzer and W. Weischedel, *Denken und Glauben: Ein Streitgespräch* (Stuttgart, 1965).

[10] Cf. J. Pieper, *Über den Glauben*, p. 58. ET *Belief and Faith.*

mathematics, and science is unsuitable because it is inadequate. The true nature and selfhood of the person can be known only if the person gives himself to be known, only if he discloses himself. He is capable of doing this because he possesses himself, because he is present to himself. The self-disclosure of the person is a free choice and decision (he could close himself off in silence), and also an act of love (he could turn aside, or feign and deceive).

Faith opens the way to the person. The believer shares in the life, thought, knowledge, perception, loves, and desires of the person who discloses himself in self-revelation. He shares in the way in which the person sees himself and the world of things and men.

The "I believe in you; I believe you" necessarily includes particulars, for it also takes on the form, "I believe what you say, what you demand, what you promise." Thus faith becomes a belief in statements, a belief in the sense of an entirely determinate and concrete sort of "acceptance" of statements and propositions which are not accessible through insight and experience, but through the disclosure and revelation of that which I believe. But this belief in "truths," "propositions," and "things" is not isolated and relationless, nor it is defenseless. It is, rather, encompassed and supported by the person in whom and whom one believes. All the individual peculiarities of the "I believe that . . ." are grounded in the power and authority, and the resulting security, of the person.

Faith, therefore, is not provisional, half-way, or inexact. It is true knowledge, a knowledge that does not have to do directly with the world, things, and objects, but with persons. This knowledge is more important and more significant than the knowledge of facts for the realization of the possibilities of human existence. It is of a different quality, of a different, and higher, degree. Thus faith is not unreliable, unfounded, and defenseless, but a certain, justified, and grounded knowledge. It is grounded in the authority and the authenticity, and thus in the insight and the knowledge, of him who is believed. These reflections show us how one-sided it is to hold that there is valid knowledge only when there is sufficient experience and insight, or when empirico-scientific verification is possible. Such limitations isolate and close off important areas of reality from our knowledge, namely, those that have to do with persons, or with man and what is uniquely human, as we find it expressed within the comprehensive horizon of history and the history of thought.

Consequently, a devaluation of faith and an acquiescence in its defenselessness can succeed only if reality is limited to matters of fact or empirical experience and if these factors are then reduced to quantity and prediction, or if knowledge is identified with the complete knowledge that takes form through logic, mathematics, or the empirical and natural sciences, with no consideration of the non-objective reality of the person. It is possible to set faith and knowledge in opposition, and even in contradiction, and then to declare the defenselessness of faith, only if the diversity and multifariousness of whatever is, is dealt with inadequately and if no consideration is given to the fact that the diversity and multifariousness of whatever is cannot be covered by a single method, but only by a diversity of ways, approaches and modes of knowledge.

Just as we have different sense organs—sight, hearing, taste, smell, and touch—to perceive the world of sensible experience, so we have different faculties of the mind to apperceive the world intellectually. We must become aware of and free ourselves from the total dominance and self-sufficiency of the merely factual, of empirical positivism, and we must also free ourselves from the fascination of the technical, in order to preserve this pluralism and in order to come to know the ways of access to the dimensions of the uniquely different reality of the person. This approach is necessary for the sake of humanity, faith, and knowledge.

It follows that faith is neither an obviously necessary, nor a defenseless, but rather a thoroughly grounded mode of knowledge. It is grounded in an act of trust and the surrender to a person which, through a self-communicating manifestation, gains participation and unity.

However, this act of trust must also be grounded. It is grounded in the *authenticity* of what is believed, that is, in the manner and method by which it justifies and vindicates its position, its authority, and its power; in the criteria whereby it demonstrates what it is, that is, in that which waits for faith and serves it. The demonstrability of this authenticity is the condition and presupposition of faith and the knowledge and awareness it includes.

Authenticity pertains to the presuppositions of faith. Therefore it is not a part of what the believer believes, but rather pertains to what he knows, or at least must be able to know. If *everything* were a matter of belief, then there would be no faith at all. No one, as Thomas of Aquin remarked in reference to Augustine's treatment of credibility (*ratio credibilis*), would (and could) believe unless he would (and could) perceive that the state of affairs to be believed presupposes credibility.[11] Credibility is chiefly a personal quality which is known in a manner similar to the way in which we come to know a person. There is here no evident, or obviously necessary, knowledge in the sense of a logical deduction, a mathematical equation, or an exact, experimental verification, but a knowledge based on different, converging facts, "signs," experiences, observations, words, and indices, which, taken individually, are perhaps insufficient, but which when taken together and assembled with the whole person in mind are sufficient to bring about a knowledge of and conviction in the credibility of a person. This activates that power in man that Newman has called the "illative sense." The question of the credibility of faith is analogous to the question of the foundations of love in the "respect for love" in any given man. At any rate, the question of credibility has to do with real knowledge, for it comes about through a confrontation with (human) reality.[12]

This fundamental process with regard to the presuppositions of faith is expressed in the well-known proverb, "Take care in whom you trust." Faith, as we have said, means to share in the knowledge of one who knows. If there is no one who sees and knows, it is impossible that there be someone who believes. Faith is made legitimate through the credibility of faith. This will occur

[11] "Nemo enim crederet nisi videret ea esse credenda vel propter evidentiam signorum vel propter aliquid huiusmodi" (*Summa theologica*, II–II, 1, 4, ad 2).

[12] J. Pieper, *Über den Glauben*, pp. 54–57.

if there is someone who is intimately acquainted with what is to be believed and if the believer has some kind of relation to this someone. We also thereby come to see that faith is grounded and is not defenseless.

III

This analysis also characterizes the fundamental structure of faith that is designated faith in a special way, namely, as *belief in God and the Christian faith.* This must be the case if such faith is intended as, and strives to be, an act of man. Thus it cannot in any way ignore the slightest aspect of what it is capable of being, otherwise it cannot be a human faith.

Something should be said, therefore, concerning the manner in which belief in God is found in man.

What we have said so far clearly shows that the radical and unlimited act of faith is not possible within the horizon and scope of the human person, no matter how strongly faith as such desires and intends it. The full realization of faith constantly founders on the intellectual and ethical limitations of humanity, that is, on the deficiencies, on the weakness and unreliability, on the extremely differentiated credibility of the person (or persons) in whom, and whom, in faith, I believe. The highest degree and intensity of personal faith is found between persons who are joined together in love. But how often, even here, is faith disappointed and unsettled through denial, narrowness, disloyalty, fickleness, and doubt? Yet they who strive for the highest perfection of self in faith and love realize most clearly, and therefore most painfully, that it is impossible to actualize faith consistently, completely, and unconditionally. Thus not only the deficient aspects of faith, but its truest and highest realization, make it clear that faith refers beyond the horizon and possibilities of intra-human relations and, as personal faith, seeks realization in a manner that is free from any kind of limitations or insufficiency.

Faith, therefore, is set free from its intra-human and interpersonal activity through that dimension in which faith attains true self-perfection. This perfection is not possible in the intra-human dimension. It is possible only where faith can be related to a personal Thou who is different from all finite personality, but who at the same time possesses more, not less, personality, that is, a Person in the absolute sense of the word, the very possibility of an unlimited "ground for myself in another." Then again, this perfection of human faith in a Personality that transcends humanity is the fulfillment of the deepest intention of faith as a human activity. Of course, it cannot be said in consequence of this conception of faith that there is or *must* be the transcendent, absolute Thou in whom faith is realized and completely fulfilled. But it can be said that if there is a transcendent, absolute Thou, then the fulfillment of the possibility of faith as such lies in belief related to that Person. For here the restrictions and limitations that determine faith as an engagement of man with man would not hold. At the same time, we can see how human, how man-oriented, how existential it is that there should be such a transcendent, personal reality and that the believing man could believe in him and there find the perfection of the meaning of his existence; and, on the other hand, how utterly frustrating and empty the deepest intentions of man are if there is no such transcendence.

Blondel's conception of the "supernatural," which is gaining influence in contemporary reflection on faith, is grounded in considerations such as these. It is, as he formulates it, a cry of human nature that no amount of self-effort can fulfill. The "supernatural" for man is something that can neither be won nor reached, but at the same time it is something that is absolutely necessary and essential for the presence and fulfillment of meaning in human existence in its highest sense.[13]

This approach is an indication of how the nature and existence of man is open for the supernatural, for God, and how they affirm this unconditioned and absolute reality, a reality that transcends the human person, in the fundamental acts of man, that is, in the limitlessness of inquiry, knowledge, and love, in the function of conscience, in the fact of freedom and responsi-

[13] Cf. H. Bouillard, *The Knowledge of God* (London and New York, 1968).

bility, and in the knowledge of the radical obligations and responsibilities of the human self. However, this transcendence does not signify an escape to some geographical beyond: the affirmation of transcendence in no way means that a particular way of looking at the world *must* be affirmed or accepted. It is important only that man has the courage to attend to the deep mystery in himself and to accept his universal openness and reference to absolute transcendence. The same holds for revelation. It is not our own product or postulate. We hear it as a word spoken to us and to our questions, to questions that we ourselves are, culminating in the question of meaning—a word spoken not by us. Revelation is an event in which we participate, but which we do not cause to happen. Nonetheless, the word and the occurrence of revelation would be rejected as a meaningless chance event, as something arbitrary and unreasonable, if the spirit of man were not so that he is a "hearer of the word"—and not only of the word that he and others speak, but the word spoken to him (who with regard to the most important aspects of his existence is "speechless") by the Thou who in his absoluteness and freedom can be known by man.[14]

Revelation, as the self-communication of the God of grace and salvation, would be a pure "extrinsicism" if man were not oriented towards salvation and grace, towards the supernatural, towards union with God, and if as an historical being he were not disposed to the possibility of an historical revelation, and anticipate it. This conclusion is valid not only for historicity in general, but for the concrete, specific history made up of situations, freedom, interaction, obligations, and decisions. Thus the historical dimension is not the "foul ditch" beyond which Lessing was unable to come,[15] not some mystifying Achilles' heel, but Christianity's proper distinction, a motif of its credibility. For the historical dimension is that which is proper to man, and whatever has to do with and is a concern of men in

[14] Cf. K. Rahner, *Hearers of the Word* (London and New York, 1968); H. Fries, "Vom Hören des Wortes Gottes," in *Einsicht und Glaube*, pp. 15–27; G. Ebeling, *Word and Faith* (New York, 1966).

[15] Cf. his essay, "Uber den Beweis des Geistes und der Kraft," in *Gesammelte Werke* VIII, edited by P. Rilla (Berlin, 1956), pp. 9–16.

freedom (and this holds true of the revelation of God in a special way) must come to him within the scope of the historical dimension.[16]

Jaspers continues to claim that the historical revelation accepted by the Christian faith violates the transcendence and freedom of God. Is it not the other way around? To hold that revelation is impossible is an improper restriction of transcendence, the imposition of an illegitimate requirement.

IV

Now we shall attempt to analyze how the belief in God is constituted.

The very statement itself shows that belief in God is primarily and basically not a relation to things, statements, and formulas, but a personal act, a relation and an engagement of the human self with the divine Thou, an engagement between the uncreated and the created person. The fundamental structure of the belief in God is of the form: I believe in you—I believe you.

With reference to the intra-human dimension of faith, the manner and means whereby I gain access to the human person have to do with the way in which I come to know the depths of the personal self. The truth of this criterion becomes all the more important the higher the person is, the more he has to say, the deeper his mystery extends, and, from the other side, the more I expect and wish to know the true nature of that person, the more I am connected with him in life and conduct, the more my existence is grounded in him and united with him. Analogously, and with even greater exactitude, this criterion holds true of God and the ways in which I can get into a position to know him. It follows, then, that access to God, to his mystery, and to his true, divine reality is possible only in the form of faith. Union with God is possible only by way of faith.

We have already referred to and described the fact that a knowledge of God is given in man as such. The fact that God can be known from the created order (see Wisdom 13: 3–5;

[16] Cf. B. Welte, *Heilsverständnis* (Freiburg–Basel–Vienna, 1966).

Romans 1: 19f.) is also true of a world that strikes us today chiefly as the world and work of man, as a "worldly world."[17] For the sake of clarity, we shall condense the world and creation to the "microcosmos," to man. "To talk about man is to talk about God" is one of Bultmann's principles. He explains what he means by this principle as follows: "In his weakness man knows of the almighty strength of God, in his question concerning what is real he knows what God demands, through his transitoriness man can speak of the eternity and infinity of God."[18] The phenomena of guilt, the question of meaning, the past, the future, and death must be approached in this manner. The deepest point at which man experiences his reference to God is in the critical and practical function of conscience (a fact emphasized by both Kant and Newman, which has been taken up anew today by Ebeling).[19] Conscience has to do with personality, but not only with our own personality or with other human persons, but with the *absolute* Person, who commands unconditionally and rules authoritatively.

Expanding our frame of reference somewhat, we must point out that the realities indicated here are lived in *religion* and in *religions*. Cosmological religions and the various religions of nature, conscience, and salvation all document the different dimensions of this revelation of God and give diverse articulation to the universal and existential reference of man to the absolute mystery that we call God.

A number of things follow from this point of view. First of all, the world and man, in his spirit and conscience, are not only given facts of nature, but the creation, and thus the revelation, of him who has created in freedom and love. The personality of God is manifested directly here, otherwise the various religions, and religious phenomena such as prayer and worship, and such phenomena also as responsibility and repentance, would

[17] Cf. H. Urs von Balthasar's essay on this topic in *Concilium* (Glen Rock: 1, 1965; London: 6, 1, p. 14).

[18] *Glauben und Verstehen* I (Tübingen, 1933), p. 155.

[19] Cf. H. Fries, *Die Religionsphilosophie Newmans* (Stuttgart, 1948), J. Schulte, "Newmans Lehre vom Gewissen," in *Newman-Studien* VII (Nürnberg, 1968); G. Ebeling, *Word and Faith*.

ultimately be neither possible nor meaningful. All the forms of prayer—of thanksgiving, praise, request, surrender—are directed to a personal, understanding Thou, who can hear and respond, who can be appealed to, and who is able to give an answer. If, however, prayer is the voice of faith, it follows that faith that lives in religions is faith that responds to the many ways in which God gives himself to be known (above all in creation, but most deeply in man). For faith is related to the person, and to the way in which a person reveals himself.

A glance at the various religions, and at religion as such, shows clearly that religions refer beyond themselves to a clearer manifestation of the word, will, intentions, and mystery of God, that is, to a clearer revelation of what is given in creation, in man, and in conscience. Consequently, religions transcend themselves towards a truer form of themselves. Indications of this fact can be found in the many deficiencies of religions: degeneration and deterioration into idolatry and magic; the proliferation into unfathomable multiplicity; accentuation of the quantitative; the bestowal of self-sufficiency upon those things which are only means and medium; crystallization into functionalism and legalism; and so on.

If God is the absolute, free, and personal ground of being, his communication cannot be exhausted in his work. He is fundamentally and essentially free for new modes of self-manifestation. And man, through his spirituality and freedom, through the unlimited openness that is evident in his ability to question, through the radical openness and demand for inquiry that cannot be satisfied by any human answer or knowledge, but rather are always left open—through all this man becomes a hearer and receiver of a new word of God.

These considerations can be carried a step farther. If God, beyond his manifestations in creation and in conscience, could be known as he is in himself—in the mystery of his inner nature and life, or "in the eternal decrees of his will" (as it is put by the First and Second Vatican Councils[20]) as they relate to the ulti-

[20] Denzinger-Schönmetzer, 3004; *Dogmatic Constitution on Divine Revelation* I, 6.

mate meaning of human existence and to the salvation and end of mankind—it would be necessary for God to disclose himself and give himself to be known in a new way. Such a thing would be done through modes of self-communication that accord with his freedom but which at the same time are open and accessible to the understanding of man.

We are not merely playing a game with pure possibility when we consider the question: "Whether God could be known in a way other than with reference to his creation" (in the sense of a purely hypothetical "as if"). This is not an inapplicable postulate posed by man, but a highly significant and deeply existential concern, and for several reasons: because man is related to this absolute, transcendent ground through his very origins, existence, and nature, and is grounded in it as his source and hope; because the revelation of God present in creation and conscience is distorted by human guilt; because the truth manifest in creation can be "held back by ungodliness" in man, as Paul says (Romans 1: 18), and thus does not gain recognition; because the image of God is distorted and mistaken; and because the word of God is twisted by the false words of mankind—"*omnis homo mendax*" (Psalm 116: 11).

Newman, with reference to this situation, describes man as one who, led by the light and voice of conscience, "is waiting for" a new, articulated, and undistorted Word, for a concrete, specific, personal self-communication of God.[21] Of course, such a "supernatural" revelation cannot be postulated in view of this existential disposition. But it can be made clear that the possibility of such a new, free revelation has to do with a question, a situation, with something existential in man, and that (to return to our main theme) faith, as a response to this revelation, is not a defenseless faith, but rather is embraced by the whole of human existence and by radical questions concerning meaning and salvation. According to the formulation given by Karl Rahner, revelation is the radical, simple, and total response of God to the one question that man poses in his very existence.[22]

[21] Cf. H. Fries, *Die Religionsphilosophie Newmans*, pp. 135–155.
[22] *Belief Today* (New York, 1967).

We can say of this revelation *a priori* that if it occurs, it can only occur in the realm of history. For history is the place for what is new, for free positing, for free activity and occurrence, as well as the field for free human decision. And the form of what is new can only be of the nature of the word. For the word is the free and living way to communicate what is new, for making a promise, for the will, for grace, for assent, for actualization. Freedom, spirit, and love are present in the word. At the same time, the word is capable of giving meaning to, and of interpreting, what happens. Finally, the word is the way in which communication can be initiated and completed—communication between God and man as well as communication between men.

V

Christian faith and witness (that is, the witness of Scripture and the enduring witness of the community of believers, the Church) speak of this "something new and supernatural," namely, of the historical and personal revelation of God in word. Man is confronted with the demands of this witness. For it is said that God has often and diversely disclosed himself, that he "spoke in times past to the fathers by the prophets, last of all in these days has he spoken to us by his Son" (Hebrews 1: 1). God revealed himself in a concrete history, in the history of a people, and he revealed himself finally in a manner that drew all previous revelations together, conclusively and unsurpassably, namely, in the Word, becoming a man in body and living among us (John 1: 14) in *Jesus Christ*. Through this final revelation of God in his Son it becomes uniquely clear that (and to what extent) this self-disclosure has a personal form.

There is a statement concerning Jesus Christ that is fundamental for our problematic: "No one has at any time seen God. The only-begotten Son, who is in the bosom of the Father, he has revealed him" (John 1: 18). Jesus Christ, therefore, is the Revealer presupposed by faith. He is the one who sees and knows. He is the witness who fulfills the conditions of possibility of faith that must be given if faith is to be both possible and grounded.

If this is so, then there can be only *one* meaningful response to this revelation, namely, the response of faith in its basic form: I believe in you, I believe you—and unrestrictedly, in the full and self-completing activity in which, as the Council declared in its *Constitution on Revelation* (1, 5): "the whole man surrenders himself to God in freedom." Everything is contained here that we find given and included in the structure of faith. In faith man gains access to the knowledge of the deepest mystery of the reality of God (which is, at the same time, man's own mystery), as disclosed to him in freedom and love. It can be gained in no other way. To believe means to participate in that which is believed, to become one with it.

If we carry this structure over to the Christian faith, which believes in the final and unsurpassable self-communication of God in Jesus Christ, it follows that faith means participation and union with Jesus Christ, to be taken up into Christ's spirit and life, or, according to Paul, "to be in Christ." If faith means the grounding of existence outside of itself, then the Christian faith means the grounding of existence in Christ. However, that is possible, meaningful, and allowable only if, ultimately, the same belongs to Christ as to God, if in Christ God himself is present, if "the fullness of divinity lives" in him (Colossians 1: 19), if Jesus is *Kyrios*, the Lord, in the same sense that we attribute Lordship to God himself.

VI

If the premiss of faith is the credibility of the person who is believed, then, likewise, we must show the *credibility of the Christian faith*, as a whole and in particular. This is an immense and comprehensive task which we cannot even so much as begin to bring to completion here. It has to do with the whole field that is taken up in the study of the foundations of faith—in so-called fundamental theology. The various questions that come to the fore in this connection concentrate and culminate in the question that initiates, fulfills, and completes whatever pertains to revelation: "What do you think of the Christ? Whose Son is he?" (Matthew 22: 42). Is Jesus Christ just one among many in the religions of humanity, or is he *the* individual, the unique Revelation of God in his Person, the Son of God in the exclusive sense, the Word become man, the Lord, the Way, the Truth, the Life, the Resurrection, the Light, the Bread, the Gateway, the Salvation, the one who says of himself, "Whoever has seen me has seen the Father" (John 14: 9)?

Jesus Christ not only asserted the claim that is grounded in the mystery of his Person, his history, his word and work. He manifested it and made it worthy of belief through his life and destiny, and through the deeds that he performed in sovereign power and freedom—deeds that manifest an absolute dependence upon God and are put forth and described in the Gospels as "deeds of power," or (especially in John's Gospel) as "signs" and "works," and which we declare to be "miracles." The significance of these signs as a testimony of the Revealer is reflected in the epilogue of John's Gospel: "Many other signs also Jesus worked in the sight of his disciples, which are not written in this book. But these are written that you may believe that Jesus is the Christ, the Son of God, and that believing you may have life in his name" (20: 30f.). Contemporary exegesis has devoted all the instruments of its historico-critical method to the interpretation of these signs and the many problems related to the determination of their facticity. With regard to this situation, we must remark parenthetically that the consequence of the fact that Scripture (and whatever is equivalent to it) is inspired is not history, but the truth. The truth can take on many forms, not only the form of history. Thus unillumined dark spots and difficulties of interpretation with regard to particular aspects of these signs and miracles do not open the way to the doubt of what is essential ("a thousand difficulties do not make a doubt," says Newman), that is, with regard to the absolute and wondrous singularity, the incomparable and irreplaceable mystery that faith, by taking up the numerous biblical statements and articulating their ultimate meaning, expresses in recognition of Jesus Christ: "true man and true God."

The crucifixion and the resurrection from the dead are the fulfillment of the life, the works, and the signs of Jesus Christ. The New Testament is the witness of faith and history to these things. The difficulties and problems posed by the texts, the different sources and modes of transmission and interpretation, are under heated and wide-ranging discussion in contemporary theology, including Catholic theology.[23] This is not surprising if the destiny of faith described by Paul in the oldest testimony of Easter depends on it: ". . . if Christ has not risen, vain then is our preaching, vain too is your faith. Yes, and we are found false witnesses as to God, in that we have borne witness against God that he raised Christ—whom he did not raise, if the dead do not rise. For if the dead do not rise, neither has Christ risen; and if Christ has not risen, vain is your faith, for you are still in your sins. Hence they also who have fallen asleep in Christ, have perished. If with this life only in view we have had hope in Christ, we are of all men the most to be pitied. But as it is, Christ has risen from the dead, the first-fruits of those who have fallen asleep" (1 Corinthians 15: 14–20).

With regard to an assessment of the testimonies of Scripture to the resurrection of Jesus from the dead, we must always keep in mind that we are dealing here with something that is proposed as entirely new, unimaginable, incommensurable, and without previous analogy, something whose only parallel is creation from nothing. "The resurrection of Christ does not mean a possibility within the world and its history, but a new possibility altogether for the world, for existence and for history."[24] Amidst the undeniable and insoluble ambiguity among the Easter narratives, we find the unique history of Easter in the historical signs of

[23] Cf. H. Waldenfels, "Ostern und wir Christen heute," in *Geist und Leben* 40 (1967), pp. 22–43; W. Marxsen, U. Wilckens, G. Delling, and H. G. Geyer, *Die Bedeutung der Auferstehungsbotschaft für den Glauben an Jesus Christ* (Gütersloh[3], 1966); W. Pannenberg, *Grundzüge der Christologie* (Göttingen, 1964), pp. 47–112.

[24] J. Moltmann, *Theology of Hope* (London and New York, 1965), p. 179.

Easter, which are grounded in the testimony of the resurrection and the Resurrected One, as presented in compelling and concentrated fashion in 1 Corinthians 15: 3–8.[25]

One thing is sure (I refer here to Günter Bornkamm): without the assurance of the resurrection of Christ, there would be "no Gospel, not one narrative, not a single epistle in the New Testament; no faith, no Church, no public worship, and no prayer in Christianity as we know it."[26] And we, as Christians, are drawn into this reality and testimony. It is the ground of our faith and hope.

All of this does not leave the question, "Who, then, is this one?" (Luke 8: 25), without an answer. There is, of course, no absolute ground and certainty to the assertion, "I know whom I believe" (2 Timothy 1: 12), but it is also not defenseless. There is the reliable ground and certainty that is given to man in the personal and existential situations of decision in his existence, a certainty that is so secure that upon it faith and the decision in favor of it can be vindicated and justified, so securely that the denial of faith can in no way be made absolutely convincing.

We are thereby led to a further point, which stands as an additional contribution to the phenomenon of the "defenselessness of faith." In the mystery of Jesus Christ, which is described as the mystery of the God-man, we find the unique, historical form that constitutes the deepest *mystery of man*, namely, radical grounding and existence in God, the unity of man in God, the truth: the more a man is present to himself, the more he is present to God; the more he is present to God, the more he is present to himself. "Jesus shows himself to be nothing other than what all men '*quodammodo*' are. All men, through their nature, are *quodammodo* united with the eternal Light, but he was so united in a fundamental, higher, and thoroughly unique manner, which the Fathers [of Chalcedon] referred to as hypostatic."[27] A look

[25] J. Kremer, *Das älteste Zeugnis von der Auferstehung Christi* (Stuttgart, 1966).

[26] *Jesus von Nazareth* (Stuttgart, 1956), p. 166.

[27] B. Welte, "Zur Christologie von Chalkedon," in *Auf der Spur des Ewigen* (Freiburg–Basel–Vienna, 1965), p. 450.

at the history of the various religions shows that this can be said of no other than Jesus Christ. No one but he can lay claim to such a thing. Even Jaspers speaks of Jesus Christ as the "highest standard among standards." He says that Jesus penetrated to the point that is nothing but "love and God."[28]

In all these things, there is certainly ample room for the free decision of man (a state of affairs that is required for the very possibility of faith). And this faith seeks total engagement, radical involvement in the Revelation, Word, and Act of God that became an event and a presence in the world and history in Jesus Christ.

In this regard, we might ask with J. Pieper, Who is the critical thinker? The one who declares that nothing can be accepted as true and valid that has not stood up under a truly exact—and where possible, a mathematically exact—test; or the one who is afraid that he might miss an element in the whole of truth, and who therefore "would rather make allowances for a less exact confirmation than to miss a possible contact with reality? Can he not also lay claim to critical thought?"[29]

The distinction between believer and unbeliever, therefore, is not a distinction between smart and dumb, or critical and uncritical, or between intellectual honesty and irrational, blind belief. It is also not a distinction between certain knowledge and defenseless faith, but rather the distinction between those men who open themselves to this new reality of God in Christ and allow themselves to be called, moved, and consumed by it—that is, those who decide in favor of it and have the courage of faith for it, who ground their life and death in it—and those who, in sceptical reservation, do not wish to decide for anything or anyone, who question everything but hold to nothing—that is, those who think it is impossible in all honesty to decide, and who have therefore made a decision, although it is a bad one.[30]

[28] *Die grossen Philosophen* I (Munich, 1957), p. 205. ET *The Great Philosophers* I–II (New York, 1962, 1966).

[29] *Über den Glauben*, p. 81.

[30] K. Rahner, "*Intellektuelle Redlichkeit und christlicher Glaube*," in *Schriften zur Theologie* VII (Einsiedeln–Zürich–Cologne, 1966), pp. 54–76.

VII

One final point must yet be covered. It is possible that many men affirm the way of faith as it has been described so far and are prepared to follow it; that they accept belief in God and his revelation, and belief in Jesus Christ, with all its implications and ramifications; but that they refuse to recognize in faith what the Church "presents for belief." This element, as we indicated at the beginning, also belongs to faith, and particularly to the Catholic conception of faith. Yet it can be shown that within the scope and history of the Church there are and have been conflicts between faith and knowledge, that the teaching of the Church and the statements of science have clashed. Did the Church not pit the obedience of faith against knowledge? Does this not renew the charge of the defenselessness of faith in a new, more intensive, and more forceful manner?

The following considerations may be posed with regard to these questions. The Church cannot be separated from the revelation of God, which culminates in Jesus Christ. The Church is not only the communion of those who believe in God and Christ, but, as the new people of God and the historically enduring witness, it is both the true bearer and subject of the Christian faith and the very content of revelation, the very object of faith. We confess, "I believe in the Church." The Church has to do with what is particular and concrete in revelation, that is, it has to do with the "I believe that . . ." The Church is the work of Jesus Christ. But this work cannot be separated from its maker. Rather, in it Christ, the exalted *Kyrios*, is actual and present in a new way—in his Spirit. In the Church, the word and work, the promise and the grace of Jesus Christ, attain ever new representation and communication, so that all men at all times can be contemporaneous with him.

Thus we come to see that the Church, through its word and action, attempts to make possible, liberate, and communicate faith in a comprehensive manner. Consequently, whoever seeks to gain revelation without or in opposition to the Church, rejects fundamentally the concrete work and will of the God who has revealed himself. He rejects the unconditional act of faith itself.

However, we also see what the function of the Church consists in, with reference to revelation and faith. It has no new revelations to proclaim, but rather has to believe, declare, preserve, protect, and proclaim the revelation transmitted through the apostles. It has to explain revelation and to make it accessible to man at each new stage of history. It must build bridges from the revelation of God to man, who is to hear this word and live by it. This result comes about not only through the teaching authority of the Church, and the necessary decisions that it makes, but also, and especially, through the living and enlightened faith, through the significance of faith among the people of God, through the charisma of a theology perfected in the Spirit.[31]

What the believing and teaching Church presents for belief does not constitute control and dominion over faith and revelation, but a service in obedience with respect to its Lord and Head, who called the Church to this service and gave it its power and strength. In this service in obedience of the Church with respect to faith and revelation, which consists in preservation, development, and explanation, Christ himself is present in his Spirit, who "admonishes" it, "establishes it in the truth," and holds it faithful to its work. However, because this service to revelation and faith is done by men, and because they do not cease to be men, that is, finite men subject to their times and situations and to their possibilities of understanding, men who remain sinners in this service, the service to truth always bears the marks of imperfection. Thus we must insist upon the fact that the faith that the Church believes in is often led into serious temptation, for which the greatest courage and conviction are required. At the same time, this faith takes on the quality of gravity, concretion, and an unconquerable "nevertheless."

However, the faith that the Church believes and presents for

[31] Cf. H. Fries, "Die Kirche als Träger und Vermittler der Offenbarung," in *Mysterium Kirche in der Sicht der theologischen Disziplinen* I, edited by F. Holböck and T. Sartory (Salzburg, 1962), pp. 1–36.

belief implies that faith involves knowledge, that is, a knowledge of the life, wisdom, and reality that were disclosed for us, and for the sake of our understanding of ourselves and our salvation, through the revelation of God in Christ, in which the Christian grounds his life and death. This state of affairs means that there can be no conflict between faith and the teaching of the Church on the one hand, and the knowledge of natural reason and science on the other—or in other words, that faith is not defenseless in this respect.

If, nevertheless, such a conflict has, in fact, occurred and threatens always to break out again, the reason can only be that we have not paid attention to the horizons of both, and that there have been misunderstandings and exaggerations as to what faith or knowledge in fact are. Thus an actual outbreak of conflict always contains an appeal and an imperative to make clear what faith and what knowledge mean, and to show whether there is a concrete question concerning the truth of faith and revelation or not, and whether a particular mode of knowledge is grounded, or only expresses an hypothesis or an opinion. This appeal, however, is joined with a call for freedom and courage, the courage of faith and freedom. This response to conflicts should not be taken as a restriction against questions, but rather as a spur to freedom in setting up the problematic and in overcoming the fear that stems from narrow-mindedness (for there is also a narrow-mindedness of faith).

Conflicts between faith and knowledge are all resolvable, however, just as the actual conflicts in history could all have been resolved. As severe as the lessons of history are in this regard, they belong to the way of faith, and to the way of man, and to the way of the Church in this life. But there is another way that leads to freedom and to possible solutions and answers, in line with the suggestions that we have attempted to present here.

Let us now return to the beginning of these considerations. We have attempted to redefine and clarify the theme of the defenselessness of faith from several angles. The upshot cannot be such a guarantee and such a protection that faith would no longer be faith, which would be the case without the elements of freedom, courage, risk, and decision that it includes. This would be wrong. But something has to be said to show that faith does not stand in the defenselessness that the unbeliever ascribes to the believer, and which the believer himself sometimes fears today. And we should in some way partake of the life that is spoken of in the well-known passage from the First Epistle of Peter: "Be ready always with an answer to everyone who asks a reason for the hope that is in you" (3: 15).

CHAPTER THREE

Faith and Conviction

I

"THE PROFESSION of faith" is a phrase that we do not find spoken loud and clear today, one that we like even less to hear, and would find strange to accept or adopt. The very idea of it arouses distinct feelings of distrust and resistance.

We are aware that "professing the faith" held a much different, and even a positive place of value in earlier times. We need only bring to mind that the Protestant Church was, and still is, noted as the "professing Church," or recall the respect that was once (and still should be) accorded the one who professes the faith, especially the martyr,[1] in the history of Christianity. The profession of faith requires courage and valor, the strength of decision and responsibility, and the will to fulfill one's obligation. When supported and promoted by an active will, the profession of faith is grounded in a mode of knowledge and conviction that is capable of articulating its content, that knows what it professes, that can define, formulate, and express what it is willing to stand up for. The profession of faith presupposes discernment and orientation in order to be ready to give an answer to anyone who wants a reason for such a profession (this is an application of the passage from 1 Peter 3: 15).

Although the word "denominational" has lost its value, this should not be construed as merely a change in nomenclature which can perhaps be repaired through a better and more relevant vocabulary. It is, rather, a significant issue in light of the

[1] Cf. N. Brox, *Zeuge und Märturer* (Munich, 1961); N. Brox and W. Seibel, "Bekenntnis," in *HthG* I (Munich, 1962), pp. 151–160; N. Brox, *Der Glaube als Zeugnis* (Munich, 1966).

facts of the case, indicating an attitude of contemporary man that, with regard to Christian faith, is both noteworthy and alarming. Another important aspect of this state of affairs is the fact that profession has been employed to excess in the past in the name of faith.

One might ask: Do we not, behind the rejection and devaluation of the profession of faith, simply conceal the fact that we can no longer know with certainty, and can no longer say precisely, what can and should be professed?—because there is no enduring content, no valid orientation; because everything is dragged along in the wake of history, relativism, and uncertainty; because apparently there is nothing that is unchanging amidst all that is changing; because everything is readjusted to a new expression through interpretation, so that we can no longer clearly see whether the same thing put in a new way does not contain an entirely different content than before?

Is not the rejection and devaluation of the profession of faith linked with a tendency to deny truth and content to thought, to lay no value on orientations (and even to reject them explicitly), to maintain the feeling of suspension amidst the imprecise, the possible, and the undecided, and to cultivate the oscillation between them in order not to have to take a clear stand, in order to be able to fall back upon the "could be," "that depends," and "it's possible"?

One might ask: Is not the denial and devaluation of the profession of faith connected with another point of view, namely, that we shrink away from fixity, that we refuse to be pinned down, to decide definitely, to accept responsibility, to make an effort, to take a chance? We would rather stay at the fringe and remain uninvolved onlookers.

If there is no content that can be articulated and expressed in the profession of faith, then there is no reason that could back up a possible decision, or that would justify an effort or a risk.

To expand upon or illustrate these thoughts, it must be said that the extreme case of a profession of faith, martyrdom for Jesus, the true *Kyrios*, and a refusal to sacrifice oneself to the Roman Caesar along with a willingness to accept the consequences that follow from this even to the surrender of one's life, was, to put it mildly, based on a misunderstanding. It could have been (one would have to argue), or perhaps even should have been, avoided through a proper interpretation and clarification. We could then say, in a parody of Martin Luther's famous statement, "Here I stand, but I can do something else."

Looking at the recent past of Germany, or at contemporary world affairs, are we to say that the sacrifices, grievances, and setbacks that many men accepted in the Third Reich, and still accept in totalitarian states, for the sake of the profession of the Christian faith, are replaceable? Would we ourselves, in the contemporary spiritual situation in the West, regard a situation at hand as dangerous and then have the courage for a decision, for a profession of faith perhaps to the surrender of life? And would we be able to say why we did it, why we became involved?

If we deny the profession of faith, do we not slip into the danger of qualifying a critical situation, or perhaps only the clarity of a statement, as fanaticism, intolerance, or narrowness; of avoiding every sort of rigor in questions of decision, or at least glossing them over; and, from a Christian point of view, of stripping so much from the content of the profession of the Christian faith that all the folly and scandal of the cross would be evaded and swept away through hermeneutics and dialogue? Are we not in danger of subtracting so much (ostensibly for the sake of what is common to all Christians, or in the witness of ecumenism) until only the barest minimum remains, some sort of humanism or human cooperation according to the empty motto, "Be nice to one another"? Would not that which is ordinarily expected of man anyway, and especially of contemporary man, be made into a critical theological principle and a measure and criterion of belief? Is not modernity, the necessity of being up to date, the highest precept of the Christian faith if it wishes to avoid all forms of danger and become a mere imitation?[2]

[2] Cf. on this question, H. Urs von Balthasar, *Wer ist ein Christ?* (Einsiedeln, 1965), and *Cordula oder der Ernstfall* (Einsiedeln, 1966).

Are we not in danger of turning dialogue into dialogism, into a third confession of faith in which anyone can speak without obligation about everything imaginable? Is there not the implication here that this kind of thing would constitute true brotherhood? Could not such an important theological position as that having to do with "anonymous Christians," bringing such an important matter into the view of faith and leading to a significant assessment of non-Christians,[3] be misinterpreted and converted into a comprehensive theological principle which would require that everything be left just as it is? In such a context, preaching as well as everything having to do with missionary work would be viewed as relative and problematic, because ways to salvation and to God are to be found everywhere. How, we would be compelled to ask, can the exclusivity and absoluteness of the Christian stance be maintained if it is linked only with intolerance and uncharitableness, attitudes which can no longer be permitted in contemporary, pluralistic society?

Are we not in danger of levelling all differences, or becoming indifferent towards them, such that profiles and contours become indistinguishable?

These considerations are posed in order that we might see, from a negative point of view, what the obvious denial and devaluation of the profession of faith today consist in, and what their immediate implications are. Consequently, the theme of our chapter—faith and conviction—is not directly described but its horizon fixed and milieu determined. If our conclusions are found to be unsatisfactory, then it will be necessary to reexamine our premiss—namely, the profession of faith as such—in a more positive light.

II

In what follows we shall consider what relation the profession of faith has to faith itself.

[3] Cf. K. Riesenhuber, "Der anonyme Christ, nach Karl Rahner," in *Zeitschrift für kath. Theologie* 86 (1964), pp. 286–303; K. Rahner, "Die anonymen Christen," in *Schriften zur Theologie* VI (Einsiedeln–Zürich–Cologne, 1965), pp. 545–554.

It is impossible to profess that the Pythagorean theorem is correct, that Caesar is dead, that Napoleon once lived. However, I can profess that Christ died "for me." It follows that one can profess only what is not self-explanatory, what is not universally evident. It is also impossible to profess what can be ascertained and known scientifically, what is so structured that it makes no difference to me that I am affected by it, interested in it, involved with it, or moved to a decision because of it. I can only profess something that can be contested and denied (and with reason), that is, something that requires conviction. I can only profess something that can be distinguished and contrasted, that can lead to opposition and contradiction. I can only profess something in which I can ground my existence, in terms of which I can live and die. Such profession is essentially and necessarily connected with faith.

The profession of faith as an activity and externalization, as the structure of what is expressed in the profession itself, is a witness to faith. The profession of faith is a sign that faith has been received and understood, that its word has been heard and can be made intelligible. However, it is very important to note that the profession of faith is not the pure voice of religious faith as such, as in religions that give diverse and complex testimony to the relationship of man to God and to things divine, but (as in the nature religions and cosmic religions) never move from there to clear expression, to historicity, and to decisiveness. Rather, they take the pantheon of the gods as their legitimate expression, a pantheon that knows no bounds nor limits to assimilation and is unendingly expandable, where everything has its place in harmony, where every form of opposition is absorbed and given voice and function. It is also characteristic of such religions that they are not bound to any time, to historical events, to any historical person, but rather that they find themselves in a circle of fixed repetition. Thus they can say of the content of their religions, "It happened nowhere, but always." There can be no profession of faith here because nothing can be clearly said.[4]

[4] Cf. H. Fries, "Mythos und Offenbarung," in *Fragen der Theologie*

The same thing is true of the great religions of the East, such as Hinduism,[5] whose deliquescent ideas of divinity, seeing all in one, and its multifarious forms of expression, never allow of unequivocal explanation or determination. Such religions are even prepared to plant Christianity as a flower in their gardens of faith, but refuse to recognize it as anything but just another flower. They have no understanding of the distinctiveness of Christianity, or of its claim for definitiveness, and even expressly resist it. As a consequence we can say that the profession of faith, as the voice, expression, and witness of faith, can be found where faith does not dissolve into, and become mixed with, the variety of religions, but rather where it articulates itself clearly, where it says something and has something to say, where it deals with historical facts, where we find historical personages as the bearers and transmitters of the faith, where faith is not the echo of its own (even if religious) self-reflection, but a response to a Word that is more than human word—a response to an historical event that man himself does not stage, manipulate, or bring about.

We find a profession of faith in the biblical religion of revelation that culminates in the self-manifestation of God in Jesus Christ, and religions which, like Islamism, stand within the horizon of this revelation. This faith, whose voice is the profession of faith, is unique in that it is characterized by authority, historicity, literature, deeds, events, interactions, and persons; in that this revelation made itself understood and manifested itself expressly, that it seeks to approach me, confront me, involve me, and call me to decision.

The fundamental form of this faith, as a response to the comprehensive Word of the self-communication of God as a

---

heute, edited by J. Feiner, J. Trütsch, and F. Böckle (Einsiedeln–Zürich–Cologne, 1960), pp. 11–43, and "Das Christentum und die Religionen der Welt," in *Wir und die andern* (Stuttgart, 1966), pp. 240–272; H. R. Schlette, *Colloquium salutis: Christen und Nichtchristen heute* (Cologne, 1965); J. Heislbetz, *Theologische Gründe der nichtchristlichen Religionen* (Freiburg–Basel–Vienna, 1967).

[5] J. A. Cuttat, *Begegnung der Religionen* (Einsiedeln, 1956); K. Klostermaier, *Hinduismus* (Cologne, 1965).

Person in history, is, as we have said: I believe in you. The horizon for the determinations and expressions of the content of faith is thereby disclosed. The contents of faith are not arbitrary or isolated declarations and formulas, but concretions of the "I believe in you."

The profession of faith, therefore, is possible only where we find faith in the true and decisive sense of the word, that is, in terms of what is declared by the Bible in the Old and New Testaments. The profession of faith, as the response of faith, is truly possible only if we actually find faith as a response. The profession of faith is *the response of the response*—the manifestation and dissemination of the response.

It is no surprise, then, that we find explicit professions of faith (as we have defined such profession here) in the Old Testament. There is the profession, "Hear, O Israel! The Lord is our God, the Lord alone!" (Deuteronomy 6: 4); there is the profession to Yahweh, who led Israel out of Egypt (see Exodus 12: 17; Deuteronomy 26: 8; Joshua 24: 2–15); there is the profession of those special events in the history of Israel which can only be determined theologically as an act of God, and which, as acts of God in the past, guarantee God's faithfulness in the present and future. The important profession in Deuteronomy 26: 5–9 (which summarizes the important dates in the history of salvation) begins with the famous words: "My Father was a wandering Aramean." In the professions to Yahweh, "the Creator of heaven and earth," we find an explicit declaration, as well as a clear renunciation of other gods and other nations.[6] Israel's choice and determination was not to be like the other nations, not to do what others do.

This trait of profession and faith was continued and intensified in the New Testament, where what was testified in faith was drawn together. We are familiar with the profession of Simon

[6] Cf. in particular, G. von Rad, *Old Testament Theology* I–II (New York, 1962, 1964). For a more current discussion, cf. "Beobachtungen zur theologischen Systembildung in der alttestamentlichen Literatur anhand des 'kleinen geschichtlichen Credo,'" in *Wahrheit und Verkündigung* I, pp. 175–212; J. Schreiner, "The Development of the Israelite 'Credo,'" in *Concilium* (Glen Rock: 2 [1966], pp. 757–762; London: 10, 2, pp. 16–21).

Peter, which ranks as one of the high points of the Gospel in response to Jesus' question: Who do you say that I am? "You are the Christ" (Mark 8: 29). We are familiar with Jesus' statement: "Whoever professes me before men, him will the Son of man, [him will I] profess before my Father in heaven [before the angels of God]" (Matthew 10: 32; Luke 12: 8). We are familiar with Paul's reflection on the attitude and content of the Christian faith: "The Word is near thee, in thy mouth and in thy heart (that is, the Word of faith, which we preach). For if thou confess with thy mouth that Jesus is the Lord, and believe in the heart that God has raised him from the dead, thou shalt be saved. For with the heart a man believes unto justice, and with the mouth profession of faith is made unto salvation" (Romans 10: 8–10). In the great hymn from the Epistle to the Philippians (2: 11), the following is given as a response to the Way of Jesus: "Every tongue should confess: Jesus Christ is the Lord." And we find in the First Epistle of St. John the Apostle: "Whoever confesses that Jesus is the Son of God, God abides in him and he in God" (4: 15).

The profession of faith, as we have already seen, contains both clear and articulated declaration and a determinate content. A further point, however, is that this statement does not describe all that is possible, but has to do with the *center*, the decisive core, of that to which faith is related and to which it responds: "Hear, O Israel, Yahweh our God is the only Lord"; "Jesus is the Christ, Jesus is the Lord."

The more involved professions of faith proceed from this core of biblical profession,[7] namely, from the so-called apostolic profession of faith according to triadic classification: in God the Father; in Jesus Christ, God's only-begotten Son, who is the Way; and in the Holy Spirit and his Work, and the later symbols of faith.

This fundamental structure has persisted even though further clarifications and distinctions were added to the fundamental declarations.

[7] O. Cullmann, *Die ersten christlichen Glaubensbekenntnisse* (Zürich, 1949).

With regard to the question: What is the significance of the profession of faith?, we can now hold to the important claim that it is the expression and the voice of faith insofar as it is related to the historical, personal, and verbal self-communication of God, that is, a faith that has content, elements, and "objects." This position, one often played down in contemporary theology, is totally legitimate and applicable if it is taken in its fundamental meaning, namely, not as a projection and objectivation of ourselves, but as that which stands over against us freely and sovereignly.[8] The profession of faith is the witness and the voice of faith, occupying the highly reflective and discerning position of knowing and giving expression to its center, and viewing everything else in terms of this center.

The profession of faith signifies that it does not have merely to do with a passing statement, but with an act of respect, worship, and praise (a point that is connected with the role of the profession of faith in the divine service,[9] as indicated in the Bible). The profession of faith praises and glorifies the God who professed himself (and still professes himself) to mankind in word and deed, through events, and most eminently in the Person of Jesus Christ. The function of the profession of faith is the divine service, the response of the community after having heard the word of God read and preached. The profession of faith is the culmination of the liturgy of the word. In the revitalized liturgy following the Second Vatican Council this profession has taken on clear structure and form.

The profession of faith signifies that faith as such, which can and must be professed, is not at all identical with religion in general or any single religion in particular; that faith has a distinctness and a uniqueness all its own; that Jesus Christ, whom faith professes, is not simply the founder of one among the many religions, such that he and his work could be replaced (as in Lessing's famous parable of the ring, where the real ring

[8] Cf. H. Gollwitzer, *Die Existenz Gottes im Bekenntnis des Glaubens* (Munich[4], 1963).

[9] H. Schlier, *Die Verkündigung im Gottesdienst der Kirche* (Cologne, 1958).

cannot be distinguished from the fake, and, as a matter of fact, had disappeared).

The profession of faith signifies a liberation from possible misinterpretations and narrow-mindedness. It also signifies a liberation from unbelief and faithlessness.

A number of things follow from all this. First of all, faith is not a private affair and cannot be made private. It is, rather, an openness to the community, in which it manifests itself. This is nothing but the other side, or the consequence, of the fact that revelation (which, as we have seen, faith, in its response, professes and bears witness to) is not a private revelation, but a revelation for mankind—for the multitudes, for everyone. Faith, as a response to the word of God, establishes the community of believers, namely, those who are called from the world through the word, which, of course, is the biblical sign of the Church.

Whoever wishes to believe, to come to the faith, must join this community of believers, that is, must be added to it (see Acts 2: 41), received into it, and brought to agreement with it. Therefore, it is impossible for me to come to the faith "through my own power and reason." I must receive and accept it from the community, which itself has received and testified to the faith by its very existence. The community, therefore, is a *creatura verbi.* The profession of faith, however, itself creates and grounds a new community, sustains it in life, and continually leads and brings it together as the community of believers, those who profess their belief. This approach, of course, does not exclude, but rather insists that the faith which is given and received, and therefore which depends on others, must be my own belief, my *credo,* through personal and existential acceptance.

The profession of faith as an elucidation and as a separation from other things presupposes that it is possible for the community of faith to find and profess this clear word—in other words, for the community of believers, the Church, to remain in the Truth, and for the Truth to remain in the Church.

The guarantee of this state of affairs is certainly the promise by Jesus Christ to remain with those that are his "all days until the end of the world" (Matthew 28: 20); the promise that the

Spirit, Advocate of Jesus Christ and all that is his, will bring us to the truth and remain with us (see John 14: 15–31). A further guarantee is the trust of the believers in the source and original profession of faith, namely, in the profession of the apostles.

At the same time, however, it is necessary for the sake of faith and the profession of belief, for the sake of the community of believers in the faith, that there be structures determined according to the sequence: believing, hearing, preaching, being sent (see Romans 10: 14f.), that is, that there be specific promises and responsibilities in the community of believers for the faith and for the sake of the faith; that there be specific signs, pastors, teachers, prophets, and guardians and keepers of the faith; that there be voices which speak of the harmony of the faith, in which the individual believer finds his faith articulated and expressed. Likewise, it must be possible (and, for the sake of faith, required) to explain, through our trust in the source and fundamentals of faith, how this interpretation or declaration corresponds to the truth of faith and is in accord with the profession of faith, and how others may stand against it and not belong within the community of believers. Thus the profession of faith is the norm of doctrine and also a principle for interpreting holy Scripture, which is itself a testimony to the faith. The same principle has already been used to distinguish Scripture from the apocryphal writings. It led to the recognition of the "connaturality," or agreement, of the Church with Scripture and Scripture with the Church. That does not exclude but rather requires the possibility that the profession of faith, without diminishing itself or its normativeness, remain open to the enduring, norm-giving norm of Scripture, through which the profession of faith is renewed, examined, deepened, and given life.

A further point is involved here. The profession of faith, which must be the expression, testimony, and voice of faith in the community of believers, must be *enduring* if the Church is to endure—if it is to live and become actualized in history. Consequently, the profession of faith is very specifically an expression of the historicity of the Church, that is, it gains clarification with regard to determinate situations and events, provocations, critical and sceptical questions, disputes, difficulties, and attacks.

The profession of faith, as also a profession of the believer, must actualize and realize itself with regard to what is given. The fact of the situation shows us that the profession of faith must stress those points specifically that are challenged or placed in question. Because such a profession is a profession of *faith*, it must be careful to protect, and not to falsify, the matter of faith, especially that which has to do with the source of faith. But it will not suffice to repeat the old formulas and vocabulary which have entered into the profession of faith in history. It is necessary for what is to endure that old truths be formulated in new and different ways so that they can be delivered to men who adhere to different conditions of understanding and who speak a different language.

The profession of faith, in the successive moments and concretions of history, has as its task the transition from past to present. It has as its task the exegesis of Scripture, so that the word of Scripture remains the true word of Scripture, but at the same time the word that stirs and lays claim to man in history with the same originality and intensity, calling him to the same decision and responsibility, that existed in the beginning (which, for mankind, should be an enduring and ever-active beginning).[10]

Thus the history of the Church is marked by the history of its professions of faith. In them we find not only faith, but understanding of faith, insight into faith, growth in faith. For it is characteristic of the professions of faith in the Church that they not only make possible a horizontal community, that is, the community of brothers in faith, but also a community in the depth dimension of history, that is, community with the fathers

[10] M. Blondel, *History and Dogma* (New York, 1965); V. Berning, P. Neuenzeit, and H. R. Schlette, *Geschichtlichkeit und Offenbarungswahrheit* (Munich, 1964); cf. K. Rahner and K. Lehmann, *Kerygma and Dogma* (London and New York, 1968); H. Fries, "Die Wahrheit des Glaubens und die Geschichte," in *Wir und die andern*, pp. 41–66; W. Kasper, *Dogma and the Word of God* (London and Baltimore, 1969), and "*Geschichtlichkeit der Dogma?*," in *Stimmen der Zeit* 179 (1967), pp. 401–416.

of the faith, who must be honored and respected because we, as historical individuals, are indebted to them and could not have been without them.

However, because the professions of faith in the Church have had to do with a real history, continuity cannot be the only element of this historical process, which would then lapse into fixations and crystallizations. Historicity also includes the emergence and future of what is ever new. This does not mean that in the profession of faith new revelations are always being disclosed, but it signifies that faith, faced with the challenges of history, gives new answers to the questions posed to it here and now. It must give them, but it also can give them. At the same time, this requirement also signifies that the profession of faith, as *norma normata*, is renewed through a constant return to its source, that is, through a deepened understanding of holy Scripture, which, as Möhler says in his work, *Die Einheit in der Kirche*, is a "source in fullness,' and which, as source, flows higher than the stream.

Thus through the profession of faith and the various professions of faith in the Church, we not only say what once was the case with the faith, but we find disclosed to us what faith is, what aspects and dimensions it possesses, what richness it displays. The historical dimension does not become a relativization of values, or a constant negation of what has already occurred, but rather becomes the comprehensive continuum in which the perspective of faith is developed, expounded, and preserved. We then see what sort of fullness the "source in fullness" contains. The historical process of faith must certainly not be viewed (in a mood of highly inappropriate triumphalism) as a never-ending advance to ever-greater perfection. The history of the faith and the Church, rather, is characterized by a dialectic of continuous and discontinuous ups and downs.[11]

This suggestion may be taken as a definite reassurance in light of the fear we have today with regard to the reductive tendencies of historicism. The solution is not to do away with this his-

[11] Cf. M. Seckler, "Der Fortschrittsgedanke in der Theologie," in *Theologie im Wandel* (Munich and Freiburg, 1967), pp. 41–67.

toricism (which would be impossible anyway), but to get to its true and undisguised form and make it our own.

Finally, the profession of faith signifies and requires that it must address itself to, and defend itself before, the public, the neutral as well as the hostile, the scientific as well as the social and political. Profession of the faith signifies that the one who so professes can be put on trial, that he must profess his profession of faith in the open, that he who professes his faith may have to endure ridicule, mockery, obstacles, injury, and, in extreme cases, punishment, persecution, and finally death, for the sake of this profession of faith. It signifies, then, that the believer becomes an open professor of the faith—that he reaches martyrdom not as if he rushed towards it as his objective (that would, according to the old teaching, go contrary to the nature and meaning of martyrdom), but that he does not evade the decision that is expected of him, and does not deny it.

He who believes and professes his belief in this way stands in imitation of what is said in the First Epistle to Timothy, that Jesus Christ bore witness before Pontius Pilate "in glorious confession" (6: 13). He takes on the mark of the forms and signs of faith described in the twelfth chapter of the Epistle to the Hebrews. He stands in imitation of him who was contradicted (Luke 2: 34), whose cross, signifying folly and scandal, represents the world's answer to God's offer (1 Corinthians 1: 23).

III

We have so far put together the premisses whereby we can address a final word to the question: What do faith and its profession signify *today*?

The profession of faith today means that if there is a faith, and that if it is to endure, we must persist in its profession—taking into account all the ramifications of such a profession, namely, a content, expressibility, obligation, responsibility, openness, a relation to the community and to authority, differentiation, and distinction.

The profession of faith today means to stand in continuity

with previous professions of faith, including the original profession of faith, in the so-called apostolic succession and tradition. The profession of faith today means that we do not have to make a fresh start, but that we are in a position to receive what is given and passed along and to make it our own. The profession of faith today means to stand in tradition. The profession of faith today does not mean to fall back in great uncertainty behind the stance of what is known and expressed in faith, but it also does not mean to repeat what is past. It means to transfer what is past into the here and now. The profession of faith today means to have courage with regard to the content and objectivity of faith. The profession of faith today means to realize that escape through renunciation of obligation is itself basically a decision. Man, fundamentally and determinately, is directed to the concrete and to obligation. He must not decide for everything, but for something concrete in life—in his vocation, in his dealings with other men, and in questions concerning God and salvation. This tendency towards concretion reflects the articulated content of faith and the Christian profession of faith; or, put the other way around, the concretion of revelation reflects the concretion of our answer in faith and its profession.

The profession of faith today also mean that we must recognize the situation in which we find the Christian faith and its Christian profession, which, through historical events and decisions, has led to the fact that from the profession of faith have come many professions, from the confession of faith many confessions, resulting in a diverse understanding of the faith—as the decision for one confession as opposed to another—that has brought about a separation in the community of faith.

The profession of faith today means to recognize that separation in the faith is of necessity in opposition to the unity of faith, that the diversity of confessions cannot be equated with the plurality of churches in the New Testament, or that this is the way in which the manifold richness of the faith is to be brought to light. We must hold to the contrary, that the light of the Gospel is thereby darkened, the credibility of faith shaken. The profession of faith means to recognize that what has happened cannot be made not to have happened, but that at the same time it can be altered precisely because it is a human event—that is, an event posed in the freedom of man. This alteration becomes a duty, then, if what has happened is something that should not have happened.

Thus the profession of faith today means to confront this disturbing situation and to attempt to change it, in the power of faith and love, and in the trust of hope.

Such a thing cannot happen through the self-appropriation of the least common denominator (which could only lead to a unification in no man's land), nor can it happen through a process of addition and subtraction (which could only lead to an intermediate area of an unclear, interconfessional Christianity, where the danger is that the profession of faith itself would be minimized as much as possible). But above all it cannot happen by playing down or concealing points of contention. This would only produce the appearance of unity without foundation.

Nevertheless, the profession of faith today cannot rest content with the boundaries and differences that have been already drawn, much less with any demand to dig the trenches deeper or build the walls higher. The profession of faith, through its various professions, has been dominated by such tendencies for too long. The profession of faith today also means to discover, amidst and behind all differences, what is common to the faith and to the Christian and ecclesiastical dimension, and to bring it into the awareness of community of faith. It means to realize the possibilities of all that is common in prayer, in hearing the word of God, in the cooperation of doing good works, in the diaconate, in the service to mankind, in common Christian witness, in the orientation of hope in opposition to fear and doubt.

The profession of faith today means to suffer with the "not yet" and the "already" that hold sway between the Christian confessions, to be tolerant in patience and faith, but at the same time to prepare for the unity of paths in the trust of hope. The profession of faith today means to respect Christian dissent, to recognize it as a question and a challenge concerning the true reality of things, and to seek a satisfactory answer.

The profession of faith today signifies above all else, now as well as in the past, the profession of faith in Jesus Christ, our Lord. It signifies a readiness to follow him. It signifies a recognition that the more we become one in him and with him (for which a daily conversion is required), the more we become unified among one another. We must strive, not for the minimum, but for the maximum of faith and love. There should be *one* concurrence between the various confessions, and not one according to proportion, prestige, or power, but rather that concurrence of greater trust and love in him whom all acknowledge as their common Lord.

CHAPTER FOUR

The Critical Function of Faith

THE JUSTIFICATION for, and necessity of, the science of faith—that is, theology—is grounded in the nature and fact of revelation, and the faith that is directed to it. The whole man (a wholeness that includes both understanding and the quest for rational explanation) is involved in the event of revelation—the free and merciful self-communication of God. If science is a precisely articulated and developed mode of understanding, that is, understanding that is conceptually and methodically refined and elaborated, then these principles already contain the possibility and necessity of theology, if theology is taken to be a reflective hearing and understanding—a hearing that gives an account of itself, an explication and elucidation of revelation.

Because faith of necessity is oriented to revelation (as the response to it), and because without the faith (of man) there could be no revelation, theology's possibility and necessity can also be explained from the point of view of the phenomenon of faith. Faith, as the other side of revelation, absorbs every human power. This means that faith is not possible without hearing, and hearing is not possible without understanding. Understanding and knowledge are not added to faith externally. They are its very elements of structure and fulfillment. In understanding and knowledge we see a higher and more intensive form of faith as such; not an abandonment and negation of faith, but rather, as knowledge in the faith, a grounding in faith which brings its most basic possibilities and requirements to realization. The coordination of knowledge and understanding to faith, viewed historically, has introduced several ideas that can serve as principles of the science of faith—namely, *intellectus fidei* (the understanding of faith) and *fides quaerens intellectum* (faith seeking understanding). Thus faith is not alienated by laying claim to scientific thought. Rather, it thereby attains its true subject matter and mode of expression. The science of faith (and by this we mean theology) is a special and intensively actualized mode of understanding in faith. Theology has to do with the interconnections and foundations of faith. Thus it lays claim to all the ramifications of historical scholarship—hermeneutics, the categories of philosophy, translation into the language of science, and the struggle between ideas and the defense of essence—in order to clarify the structures of its meaning and to gain an understanding of its foundations. Theology, therefore, brings what is disclosed in the understanding of faith into relationship with the understanding which man in every historical period has of himself, his being, and his world.

I

The critical function of the science of faith, as we can see from what has already been said, is intrinsically given with faith. "Critical function" is just another way of saying "science." It has to do with the kind of thinking that judges, differentiates, completes, grounds, and sets the focus for understanding.

Because faith (not to mention the science of faith) fundamentally and essentially fits into an ecclesiastical setting and fully realizes itself only in the community of believers, that is, in the Church, the critical function exercised and undertaken legitimately by theology cannot be oriented against the faith and the Church. It cannot, therefore, be understood as an attack, an anti-religious act, or an anti-ecclesiastical position, for which one would have to be admonished in the name of faith and the Church for not having believed enough.

Thus we must reject, fundamentally and apriorily, the fear or image sometimes found today that theology and the theologian stand restrained and at a distance "over against" the Church, or situated entirely outside of it, as if the theologian were using his science as a "weapon" against the Church. Theology, as the science of faith, is possible only within the Church. The theologian properly and adequately understands himself and his task only if he conceives it as a function in the Church, and works it out within the limits of the Church, in *medio ecclesiae*.[1]

Actually, every believer is a theologian, or at least should be. Every believer should be able to give an account of his faith, in accordance with the command, "Be ready always with an answer to everyone who asks a reason for the hope that is in you" (1 Peter 3: 15). Hope is the fruit of faith, or its future dimension, although faith and hope are by no means simply exchangeable. *Spero, ut intelligam*, is not entirely identical with *credo, ut intelligam*, however much the theology of hope, as advanced by Jürgen Moltmann,[2] is a hope for theology. However, it is not possible to render an account, to give an answer, without a critical perspective (this is also Paul Tillich's understanding of the task of theology[3]).

Recognizing that every believer, for the sake of his belief, must appropriate the faith to himself in his own way, and bring it within the horizon of his existence and understanding, theology stands as a real concern, as a valid stance, as a vocation, a gift, and a task. The theologian seeks, or should seek, to take up in a special way what is enjoined of all believers. Doing this works to the advantage of the faith of everyone, that is, to the advantage of the Church as the community of believers. Theology is actively concerned with probing into faith, or, as Söhngen puts it, with "understanding in faith."[4]

The attempt to attain understanding, as we have seen, takes

[1] On the structure of theology, cf. H. Fries, "Theologie," in *HthG* II, pp. 641–654; B. Welte, "Die Wesensstruktur der Theologie als Wissenschaft," in *Auf der Spur des Ewigen*, pp. 351–365; G. Söhngen, "Die Weisheit der Theologie durch den Weg der Wissenschaft," in *Mysterium Salutis* I, pp. 905–980.

[2] J. Moltmann, *Theology of Hope*, cf. H. Fries, "Die Hoffnung als Prinzip der Theologie," in *MThZ* 17 (1966), pp. 265–267, and below, Chapter Five, "Faith and Hope."

[3] Cf. P. Tillich, *Systematische Theologie* I (Stuttgart², 1956), pp. 9–83; II (Stuttgart, 1958), pp. 19–22. ET *Systematic Theology* I–II (New York, 1967).

[4] G. Söhngen, *Philosophische Einübung in die Theologie: Erkennen-Wissen-Glauben* (Freiburg–Munich, 1955), p. 95.

place in a number of ways: as the concern for the elucidation of the inner coordination and inter-connectedness of the contents of faith; as a concern for the representation of the historical continuity of faith; as an indication of the tight connectedness of past, present, and future; as a comprehensive and critical interpretation of the sources to which faith is related; as transmission and communication; as the coordination of faith and its contents to the world-view, the spiritual stance, the scientific experience, the questions and problems, and the understanding of existence of man as he lives in history and projects himself into the future. All of this is accomplished not by faith as such, as pure hearing, as *fides implicita*, but by faith as it critically inquires and is itself questioned and challenged. Questions and answers can be given only by faith that has expanded into an understanding of faith, that is critical and differentiating—by, in other words, self-examining faith.

As Emil Brunner has pointed out, the perception and acceptance of such a task, the "employment of thought," demands specialization and the division of labor. For it is neither necessary nor possible that everything be done by each. That does not mean that whatever is done by individual theologians is of advantage to the whole, to the totality of faith. Rather we are referring to the principle of representation, the universal law of "for one another" properly understood.

II

In order to see the task and meaning of theology in the Church more clearly, it must be said that theology today, with respect to its unique vantage point, has to do with the vocational development of those aspects of the Church which involve the task of preaching, interpretation, and instruction, as well as those aspects of the Church which are invested with an office (especially that of leadership and direction) which is obliged with guarding and protecting the faith. Here we face a concrete difficulty. If the believer is already a theologian, that is, one who reflects upon his faith, who answers for it and gives an account of it, then whoever has a special service to the faith, as deacon, preacher, minister, clergyman, pastor, bishop, and so forth, should be a lifelong theologian.[5] It cannot be denied that there have been, and still are, such people. But this coincidence is by no means self-explanatory. In the majority of cases there is today a sharp division of labor and function between theology and the so-called practical ministry—a situation that is often the cause of friction and tension. For example, pastors often claim that they do not even know where to begin with theology, that it is too abstract, too alien from reality. Or (and this is the case met with most frequently today) they say that they can no longer afford to be concerned with theology, to read learned and difficult theological treatises which in this day and age are quaint preparation for the public ministry. Yet experience has shown that when preaching and instruction (the ministry's two most important tasks today) are inadequately grounded in their theological root they become mere motion and activism. We cannot separate the goal from the way thereto.[6] On the other hand, theology is also at fault if, under some ill-conceived guise of "objectivity" or "perspective," it does not keep before its view the everyday concerns of the pastoral ministry, and strive to answer the questions of existential man in the concrete language of faith.

Yet, while theology is often criticized for having no real understanding of the realities of life, it is also suspected by the teaching authorities of being too critical, too problematic, too

[5] This point raises the question concerning the proper education of theologians and the training of pastors. Cf. H. Fries, "Die theologischen Studien: Stand und Hoffnungen," in *Begegnung der Christen*, edited by M. Roesle and O. Cullmann (Stuttgart–Frankfurt, 1959), pp. 527–545; K. Rahner, *Nature and Grace* (London and New York, 1964); and "Uber die theoretische Ausbildung künftiger Priester heute," in *Schriften zur Theologie* VI (Einsiedeln, 1965), pp. 139–167; and "Theologenausbildung im Umbruch," in *ThGl* 56 (1966), pp. 1–81 (special edition); L. Waltermann, ed., *Klerus zwischen Wissenschaft und Seelsorge* (Essen, 1966).

[6] Cf. M.-D. Chenu, "Tradition und Soziologie des Glaubens," in *Kirche und Überlieferung*, edited by J. Betz and H. Fries (Freiburg–Basel–Vienna, 1960), pp. 266–275; H. Stenger, "Wünsche an die Wissenschaft," in *Lebendige Seelsorge* 13 (1962), pp. 153–157; J. Trütsch, "Theologische Wissenschaft in seelsorgerlicher Verantwortung," in *ibid.*, pp. 162–170.

disturbing and perplexing: too bent on shaking the deep-set foundations of faith. What (it is asked) has meaning any more? Everything is becoming uncertain: what remains? To safeguard against this theological ravage it is demanded by some members of the magisterium that the theologian stand "within the Church," that he be bound by the authoritative and definitive decisions of the teaching Church, since Christ gave his word and work over to his apostles and their successors, to the *cathedra Petri*, and not to professors. It is maintained that in case of conflict, whenever a decision is required, it is not the theologian, but the bishop (that is, the college of bishops, with the pope at its head) that has the final and authoritative word. As a hope and consolation, it might be added that the current situation, due chiefly to the Council, will certainly pass, so that although we find ourselves now in a period of change and transition, the time will soon be here when we shall once again have firm ground beneath our feet. However, the present situation demands of us not to *get through* this period of crisis as quickly as possible but to *get into* its risks and tasks, as urged by the Council.

Consequently, there is a rather considerable difficulty regarding the position, task, and function of theology today, namely, whether it is so limited by the constitution and structure of the Church, and by the distinct responsibility for the faith set aside for the bishops, that one should no longer speak of specific and legitimate theological claims, but rather of auxiliary services, of subordinate, restricted, and clearly defined functions.

III

We can get a clear picture of this approach to theology by recalling that there was (and to some extent still is) a theology that took the "use of thought" in the Church to mean the acceptance of the promulgations of the teaching authority (as they are found published in dogma, council documents, and papal encyclicals, which, for the most part, are ponderous, global, and undifferentiated in form) as the starting point, the source, the norm, and the measure, which were to be interpreted literally (never critically or historically) and shown to be corroborated by Scripture and tradition. The result of such efforts should turn out to be that whatever is confronted in the present (but never questioned or discussed) can be understood as the legitimate presentation, development, and actualization of the fundamentals that remain unchanged in history.[7]

Quite a few theology textbooks exhibit this basic structure. Their starting point is dogma, or Church doctrine, variously qualified theologically; followed by a grounding of what has been presented in the documents of faith and revelation, namely, in Scripture and tradition (that is, the testimony of previous doctrinal decisions, professions of faith, liturgies, Church fathers, and great theologians, as signs of this faith).

Now it should in no way be denied that the dogma and doctrine of the Church stand in a continuum with the sources and history of faith, or that this continuum must be authenticated and that this authentication is a legitimate and necessary task of theology. But no one will deny that this authentication is not always easy to handle. History, and thus the history of faith, is an extremely intricate interweaving of many aspects in which "that which is distinctly Christian" and the "hierarchy of truths" have not always been clearly preserved. It is precisely such a situation that must be avoided today, but that is not possible without a theological ability to distinguish, that is, without criticism, which has a sense for theological proportion and the historical, categorical, and terminological significance of the matter at hand, and seeks renewed actualization as well as localization and relevance. Relevance depends on numerous historically conditioned and hence unstable factors stemming from society, culture, and learning. It would be an exercise in triviality to supply historical evidence for the continuity of faith without taking account of the various signs of discontinuity—yet this was the perspective of Cardinal Manning, John Henry Newman's antagonist: that dogma orders history.[8]

[7] For a critique of this approach to theology, cf. G. Söhngen, *Der Weg der abendlandischen Theologie* (Munich, 1959).

[8] Cf. (I. Döllinger), *Römische Briefe vom Council von Quirinus*

It should also be asked whether theology must approach its subject matter with this unvarying form and method, or whether there might not be different approaches which would be more suitable to the times, and should therefore be followed.

In many contemporary treatments of Catholic theology, beginnings have been made at points urged explicitly by the Council: that themes are to be traced back directly to their biblical sources; that an historical overview should show how sources have been taken up into the growth and development of faith, and into its changing structures and forms; and finally, that consideration should be given to the systematic question concerning how the fundamental aspects of faith, through their development in history, manifest the very matter at hand and bring it into focus.[9]

If theology were to view its subject matter as merely the corroboration of what has been promulgated by the teaching authority, if it were only an interpretation of Denzinger, if its only concern were to become an "encyclical theology" or a theology of the Council and conciliar texts, then we could not speak of a critical function of theology, but only of claims that have been made upon theology.

IV

As we have already said, it is certainly legitimate that claims should be made upon theology, for theology is in the service of the community of believers. But if theology's only concern were to institute a corroboration of the factual, and a foundation for the practical, and wherever possible of the *status quo*, it would

---

(Munich, 1870), p. 61. The declarations of *Deputatio de Fide* indicate how this approach was refuted as well by the First Vatican Council; cf. *Coll. Lac.* VII, *Sp.* 287d. 288a; cf., on the other hand, Lord Acton's statement several years previously: "God's handwriting exists in history independently of the Church, and no ecclesiastical exigence can alter a fact" (John Emerich Edward Dalberg-Acton, *Essays on Freedom and Power*, edited by G. Himmelfarb [Boston, 1949], p. 280).

[9] This perspective is drawn from the *Handbuch theologischer Grundbegriffe* (Munich, 1962–1963) and from my work, *Revelation*, previously cited.

be an extremely deficient and highly questionable enterprise. This would confirm the suspicions of those who mistrust theology as an ideology. However, as a mode of thought which has nothing to do with the elucidation and explanation of reality, or with the knowledge of truth, but rather is placed in the service of specific interests and aims, ideology is the complete opposite of faith.[10] Theology must not only bring the (legitimate) claims imposed upon it to completion; it must satisfy its own claim in the performance of its function.

This point of view is intimately connected with the fact that the Church cannot simply be concerned with protecting and guaranteeing the faith by limiting its contents and bounding them off with definitions. More basically, the Church should take it upon itself to revivify and renew the faith, to fill it with new aspiration, to make the faith both credible and contemporary, and to disclose the future horizon that it contains. To this end it does not suffice simply to corroborate the facticity of what has been, and neither does it suffice (which could be extremely dangerous) simply to repeat literally what has already been formulated (possibly in false terms), so that faith and its contents could be fixed once for all and participate in (or anticipate) the finality of eternity. Whoever thinks so overlooks the uniqueness of the truth of revelation and faith as manifested in the Bible, which is more than a judgmental or propositional truth, and something other than the epiphany of the content of a timeless essence. That does not mean that the truth of faith goes against other modes of truth, but it does make it necessary for us to take note of the differences between them. The truth that is uttered in faith actualizes verbally the unattainable mystery of God and his word, his free self-communication, his living work, his historical actions and advent, which "established" this truth and at the same time disclosed the future as the fulfillment of the promises of faith.[11]

[10] Cf. Chapter Six, "Faith and Ideological Thought."

[11] Cf. W. Kasper, *Dogma unter dem Wort Gottes*, pp. 58–109; H. Fries, "Die Wahrheit des Glaubens und die Geschichte," in *Wir und die andern*, pp. 41–66.

Faith is determined by these fundamental elements as a response and confrontation. It is related to the truth disclosed in the self-manifestation of God, and is grounded through participation in the (specific) truth and obligation that it contains. We also find here the basic characteristics of such a faith—it is "that which is imperfect," "a glance through a glass darkly," not "face to face" (1 Corinthians 13: 10–12), "a strong assurance of things to be hoped for, the evidence of things that are not seen" (Hebrews 11: 1).

Because faith, as a response, is a possibility bestowed upon (historically existing) man, it is included directly in the dimension of the historical and the finite. Thus it proves to be the continuance of being in process, as a preparation that is never completed and can never be drawn to completion. The enduring truth of faith is not endangered or denied through historicity, rather it is brought closer to itself. The process of history brings to the "fullness of time" what has come to pass through the presence of the word, the truth, and the love of God, and what is to be brought to perfection in the future.

The Church, therefore, as the community of believers, is understood correctly if it is taken to be the wandering people of God, who are grounded in Jesus Christ, who came and will come again, who is the beginning and end of the Way, Alpha and Omega. Both the obligatory and irrevocable nature of the faith of the believing Church, and its openness, dynamism, and future-directedness, are reflected in this realization.[12]

The critical function of theology should be determined in light of these considerations. Accordingly, it should consist in the fact that the specific and differentiated understanding of the truth and development of faith becomes active and present, with

[12] Cf. R. Grosche, *Pilgernde Kirche* (Freiburg, 1938); R. Schnackenburg, *God's Rule and Kingdom* (London and New York, 1968), and "Kirche und Parusie," in *Gott in Welt* I, edited by J. B. Metz, W. Kern, A. Darlapp, and H. Vorgrimler (Freiburg–Basel–Vienna, 1964), pp. 551–578; W. Joest, "Die Kirche und die Parusie Jesu Christi," in *ibid.*, pp. 536–550; K. Rahner, "Kirche und Parusie Christi," in *Schriften zur Theologie* VI, pp. 348–367; R. Guardini, *Die Kirche des Herrn: Meditationen über Wesen und Auftrag der Kirche* (Würzburg, 1965), pp. 93–105.

all the functions and tasks that stand in the service of the faith, in the believing, professing, teaching, and ministering Church. Thus, solely in terms of what it is itself, it refuses to admit an inadmissible triumphalism in matters of faith and doctrine, that is, a misconceived, *non plus ultra* "infallibility" with regard to dogmatic decisions, or an improper claim for the omniscience of faith (which is a contradiction of faith[13]). A wide field opens up here for the critical task of theology with reference to the past and the future, one that it cannot avoid in light of its concern for the veracity and credibility of faith. The only disloyalty would be an unillumined narrowness which would be injurious to the faith itself.

The definitive, dogmatic declarations of the believing and teaching Church, which come forth from a deep inner engagement, are an expression of the irrevocable and obligatory nature of the word of God, undeniably and ultimately present in Jesus Christ, given and received in revelation. They stand under and serve the word of God (something that is expressed unmistakably in the Council's *Constitution on Divine Revelation* [II, 10]). Therefore, they must remain open and transparent for a deeper appropriation and more intensive confrontation with his word, a renewal that is both possible and necessary. This renewal occurs concretely in ever new, open, and obedient attention to the normative (and thus critical) norm given in the testimony of holy Scripture—which, according to the Council, "because it is inspired by God and written down once for all times, communicates the unchanging word of God itself and makes the voice of the Holy Spirit heard in the words of the prophets and the apostles" (VI, 21).

Because the believing, teaching, and defining Church exists historically, its dogmatic decisions, aimed at concrete situations and challenges, bear the marks of history. They are put forth in the vocabulary and categories of a specific epoch. The fact that

[13] Cf. K. Rahner, "Grenzen der Amtskirche," in *Schriften zur Theologie* VI, pp. 499–520; H. Fries, "*Ex sese, non ex consensu ecclesiae,*" in *Volk Gottes*, edited by R. Bäumer and H. Dolch (Freiburg–Basel–Vienna, 1967), pp. 480–500.

these decisions of faith and doctrine give a definitive, valid, and binding answer to an historical experience, and, insofar as it is a question of "what was said" and "what was meant," must be interpreted in this context, does not prevent it from becoming the beginning of a new phase in the history of the understanding of faith wherein further dimensions, aspects, and realities of the truth of faith appear and are disclosed. The history of the Church, as a community of believers, itself requires that, for the sake of the enduring truth and continuity of the faith, what was said definitively in the past must be said differently now if the horizon of understanding and the structure of language have changed in history; that the same meaning can no longer be conveyed with the same words if these words are no longer used in the same way. Likewise, theology must take into critical account that not only is the material completeness of the Church's declarations of faith important, but that a constant, living awareness remains for their qualitative proportion, for the core and periphery of revelation, for the *hierarchia veritatum* (as taken up in the *Decree on Ecumenism* [II, 11]) which, in its different forms of relation, lies at the base of the Christian faith. This base is given in Jesus Christ, who, as the *Constitution on Divine Revelation* says, is "the Mediator and the Fullness of the whole of revelation" (I, 2). In this way it is possible to free the individual declarations of faith from possible detachment and resulting isolation, to make them transparent at their critical (Christological) core, to gain a comprehensive integration, and thereby to gain a true understanding while avoiding alienation.

Finally, theology must also reflect on whether a possible dogmatic definition of the "total interstructure" of the body of Christ is desirable in truth and love, a problem which, with regard to the fact of a Christendom separated in faith, ecumenical endeavors, and the challenges and claims put upon the Christian faith as such, is of considerable importance and calls for deep responsibility.

These considerations, expressive of a theology aware of its critical function, are something other than (as we occasionally hear today) a grasp of the "substance of faith." On the contrary, they place the life and the renewed strength of faith in the light. They give no grounds for resignation or alarm, but rather for perfection, with the trust that comes from the truth, freedom, and hope of faith.

Furthermore, theology not only has to reflect on what has actually happened in the past and which would otherwise be disregarded; it must also *think things out* for the Church, for the believing and teaching Church. It cannot do this merely in retrospective repetition. It can accomplish this end by reflecting on the untarnished uniqueness, the enduring essential form and core of the Christian faith; by grasping the intellectual situation and projecting its further development into the future; by inquiring into the consequences that can be expected for the faith. Theology must take up questions that are actually and concretely posed with regard to the contents of faith. It must address itself to these questions and focus on the reality of the world as it is comprehensively disclosed today, and actualize as accurately as possible the "contemporary intellectual situation" so that it can introduce into that situation the reality of faith.[14]

However, the claims for theology do not simply limit themselves to the question of understanding faith in its confrontation with what is contemporary. Rather, they also are directed at *action* and *procedure*. This is the place for the contemporary emergence of "operative" or "political" theology, which has to do not merely with the understanding, clarification, or realization of faith in individual men, but with activity initiated and inspired by faith and directed at the structure and condition of the world and society. Thus we must ask critically whether historically developed social or political actualities and obligations, whether previous ecclesiastical modes of relation, organizational forms, institutions, and modes of action, can always be defended purely and simply in a changing and pluralistic world; whether

[14] Cf. J. Ratzinger, "Theologia perennis? Über Zeitgemässheit und Zeitlosigkeit in der Theologie," in *Wort und Wahrheit* 15 (1960), pp. 179–188; B. Welte, "Ein Vorschlag zur Methode der Theologie heute," in *Auf der Spur des Ewigen*, pp. 410–426; H. Fries, "Gefragtes Christentum: Antworten von gestern auf Fragen von heute," in *Wir und die andern*, pp. 339–357.

these things are necessary, irrefutable, permanently valid, or historically conditioned and variable expressions of faith; whether it is sufficient, or even allowable, to hold at any cost to positions that were once historically required even though subsequent developments have gone farther—all this prompting the pastors of the Church to submit, or acquiesce, with the stereotyped formula, "The Church has always . . ."[15]

This is the beginning of the distinction between ideology and faith undertaken by historical and systematic theology—namely, de-ideologization, de-mythologization, and de-sociologization. In the long run, the result will be a great liberation (for an example, consider the forfeiture of the Church States[16]), leading not to resignation and passivity, but to new possibilities and realizations. What at first glance will seem to be a loss of position will become a gain for anyone who has the power of discrimination, who does not let his sense for what is real become dulled, who does not strive after victory but seeks to serve the kingdom of God, which has nothing to do with power and assertiveness, but with faith and witness. We might ask: Would it not be better to think prospectively, and to draw the process of development together through a greater presence, whereby the Church could verify its claim to be the light of the world and could deny the constant reproach of having become dead weight, not only verbally, but factually? To this end, not only is a practical or political stance required, but a critical deliberation, theological, not strategic, whose concerns are larger than not to lose face or prestige.

We have said that the critical function of theology consists in the fact that it has not only a reflective but a projective function. This characteristic is grounded in the fact that the Church is not merely concerned with the maintenance and preservation of

[15] This formula, as the context indicates, also brings directly to mind the Second Vatican Council's decree on the Eastern Churches.

[16] Cf. H. Tüchle, "Kirchenstaat," in *LThK*² 6 (1961), pp. 260–265; for the situation in the nineteenth century, cf. particularly R. Aubert, *Le pontificat de Pie IX* (*1846–1878*) (Paris, 1952), pp. 80–97; N. Miko, *Das Ende des Kirchenstaates* I–II (Vienna–Munich, 1962–1967).

faith, but (without endangering it) with its actualization, vivification, and renewal.

V

In this section, we shall deal with the historical circumstances surrounding the fact that the great movements and progressive revolutions which have taken place in the Church this century have stemmed from the initiatives and impulses of a theology that is not satisfied with what exists and has happened, but rather has taken stock of its critical function.

The liturgical movement is clearly linked with theological breakthroughs into the structure of the divine service, with the concern (bred of historical research and systematic elucidation) to move from the periphery to the center, from the many to the one, and to propose in practical terms what its complete subject matter is composed of. This movement was not always in complete harmony with the instructions of Church authorities, but it nevertheless succeeded. Today such a temperament is referred to as creative disobedience, or prospective obedience.

The biblical movement also derived its critical impulse from theology, that is, from the dignity and singularity which it reserves for Scripture over against all other literary documents in the course of the history of the Church (theology, of course, is not alone in this regard). From theology, therefore, came an explicit encouragement to take up and elucidate Scripture without the constant fear of falling into misunderstanding or abuse. Of course, these dangers are possible (where are they not?). They must be confronted and drawn into the open within theology itself in courage and freedom. But even more important than the fear of abuse is the encouragement to live in the word of Scripture, and to let it become a light on the byways of human existence.[17]

The ecumenical movement, of course, is also conditioned by

[17] Cf. H. Fries, "Die Bedeutung der Heiligen Schrift für die Kirche nach katholischen Verständnis," in *Zur Auferbauung des Leibes Christi*, edited by E. Schlink and A. Peters (Kassel, 1965), pp. 28–40.

other circumstances, such as continuing struggles within Christianity as such, and the necessity for cooperation between the various denominations at all levels. However, the ecumenical movement is by no means pragmatically conditioned, otherwise it would cease once external conditions have changed. The fact that the ecumenical movement persists and grows is largely the fruit of theology, which introduced a new understanding of the Reformation and the Reformers. They were no longer simply viewed in the mirror of the Council of Trent (or, even more one-sidedly, in the mutual polemics that had crystallized into stereotypes); rather, an attempt was made to understand them in terms of their historical circumstances and theological concerns.[18] Thus the ecumenical movement, as an enduring fact, is the fruit of biblical and systematic reflection on the Church.[19]

The same thing holds for the revolution of the laity, which cannot be explained in terms of situations of necessity and crisis. It is also the expression of theological endeavors—comprehensive studies (such as Congar's) on the role of the laity in the Church—which were worked out and documented biblically as well as historically.[20] We find here not merely an harmonious unfolding and development of the biblically grounded doctrine of the people of God, but also the exposure of a long-standing stagnation, one-sidedness, and alienation brought forth by a biased and narrow concept of the Church that was in need of, and was ready for, liberation.

These concrete examples are not intended merely to draw the past into the present, and to justify thereby the completed critical function of theology that we find there. They also contain a vindication for the present and future, for a renewal of

[18] This is particularly true of criticism on the character and theology of Luther. Cf. O. H. Pesch, "20 Jahre katholische Lutherforschung," in *Lutherische Rundschau* 16 (1966), pp. 335–352; K. Forster, editor, *Wandlungen des Lutherbildes* (Würzburg, 1966); for the general problematic, cf. J. Brosseder, *Ökumenische Theologie: Geschichte—Probleme* (Munich, 1967).

[19] Cf. H. Küng, *The Church* (London and New York, 1968).

[20] Y. Congar, *Lay People in the Church* (London and New York, 1965); E. Schillebeeckx, *et al.*, "Die Laien in der Kirche," in *De Ecclesia* II, edited by G. Baraúna (Freiburg–Frankfurt, 1966), pp. 269–348.

the Church, which, in the name of renewal, is directed to the maintenance of a critical theological function, a Church whose task is to make theological knowledge fruitful in the proper manner.

VI

We are led immediately to another point. The intentions of the Second Vatican Council—aggiornamento, renewal, openness, dialogue, themes such as ecumenism, tolerance, religious freedom, non-Christianity, atheism, "the Church in the world today," the (although still very cautious) admission of common guilt, the resulting doctrine of the Church on revelation, various statements on the work of God—all of these things would not have been possible without the foregoing theology and its decisive, critical breakthroughs. This situation holds as well as for the new determination of the relationship between Scripture and tradition,[21] and for reflection on service to faith as the most important service of the ministry today,[22] and for countless other critical endeavors. And the very procedure of the Council—its declarations and conclusions (which also contain what was not said)—would not have been possible without the intensive work of the theologians of the Council in cooperation with the bishops.

Thus, according to one report, when a Cardinal exclaimed that the Church had suffered through the Council at the hands of the *periti*, he received this response from one of his colleagues: "No wonder—an examination of conscience is always painful."

[21] Cf. J. R. Geiselmann, "Das Missverständnis über das Verhältnis von Schrift und Tradition und seine Überwindung in der katholischen Theologie," in *Una Sancta* II (1956), pp. 131–150; "Das Konzil von Trient über das Verhältnis der Heiligen Schrift und der nicht geschriebenen Traditionen," in *Die mündliche Uberlieferung*, edited by M. Schmaus (Munich, 1957), pp. 123–206; "Tradition," in *HthG* II, pp. 686–696; and *Die Heilige Schrift und die Tradition* (Freiburg, 1962); Y. Congar, *Tradition and Traditions* (London and New York, 1966); K. Rahner and J. Ratzinger, *Revelation and Tradition* (London and New York, 1966).

[22] Cf. F. X. Arnold, *Dienst am Glauben* (Freiburg, 1958); *Grundsätzliches und Geschichtliches zur Theologie der Seelsorge* (Freiburg, 1949); *Seelsorge aus der Mitte der Heilsgeschichte* (Freiburg, 1956); and *Wort des Heils als Wort in die Zeit* (Trier, 1961).

If it should be asked what the significance and critical function of theology at the Council consisted in, it would certainly include the fact that thinking was focussed on biblical sources, and on the core and totality of faith; that "the hierarchy of truths" was regulative; that a distinction was made between the core and the periphery; that attention was drawn to proportion and concentration, rather than to quantity and summation, and even less to matters of surface and profile; that theological isolation was avoided; that the statements and practice of the Church were examined in the light of Scripture; that a search was undertaken for a language that can be understood today; that there was a concern for the process of communication and transmission for men and Christians living today; that the conditions and difficulties of understanding were taken into account, concerning which much has yet to be said. Of course, these efforts were not all entirely successful. But no one will deny that all of this was attempted, and that much of it was attained. However, this should not be taken to mean that whatever is demanded of man, or of contemporary man, should be made into the measure of theology. But it does mean that unnecessary difficulties should be torn down and real assistance should be offered whereby the decision of faith can be made possible with regard to the blatant scandal of the cross.

Another function consists in the fact that the Council theologians did not blindly attach themselves to historically developed and conditioned formulas, but questioned their meaning and their intentional structure, and also inquired into what stands over against man in history as he confronts it—the concrete problematic—and thus came to know the various aspects and perspectives that need to be integrated into a comprehensive theological statement. This point is connected with the distinction between matter at hand and language, content, and form—problems which are posed as legitimate questions, and which open up a broader field for the critical work and function of theology.

With regard to the critical function of theology, as well as exegesis, the dogmatic *Constitution on Divine Revelation* declares, "The task of the exegete is to work towards a deeper grasp and explanation of the meaning of holy Scripture, so that the judgment of the Church might mature on the foundation of scientific studies" (12). Without a doubt, this is a different function than the *post factum* recognition of the obvious.

The final decision, of course, on whether and when a decision is to be fixed lies not with the theologian but with the authority of the Church—that is, with the bishops and the college of bishops. But this decision is not independent of that which was worked out theologically—namely, that which is expressed and obtained by responsible, critical, and, most importantly, self-critical labor. Theology has much to do here with regard to its own tasks and possibilities, with regard to the bold and open discussion of its problems, which, through internal criticism, are brought ever nearer to a correct proportion and comprehensive perspective without need of authoritative intervention. This theological labor can perhaps also provide another service, namely, to protect against rash or hasty decisions and to allow the process of maturation and clarification to deepen. The fact that many questions were left undecided at the Second Vatican Council, or were left open, is not the worst sign for the effectiveness and the critical function of theology, which was inclined to be unpretentious. The fact that today we find not only an *ecclesia docens,* but a listening, questioning, learning, and even an *ecclesia dubitans,* is not a disconcerting or disheartening situation. In it we find represented the true mystery of faith in the community of believers.

VII

It has been pointed out many times that the intensive cooperation between theologians and bishops, which was accompanied by much trust in the Council and led to so many favorable results, has not been evident to the same extent following the Council. More concretely, the bishops, once at home following the Council, have no longer called for the advice of theologians. We should not, however, draw broad conclusions from this situation, for we must also take into account the fact that such consultation pertains to the *exercitium*, the realization, of the Council, and to the resolution of the problems that still remain, whereby what has been initiated in the post-Council period will not be set aside, but pushed forward, in the Council's name. In view of the difficulties of preaching (the central theme of the Christian faith); in view of the diversified intellectual situation, the complexity of the problems, the manifold pluralism,[23] and critical reflection; in view of the sought-for dialogue with the world, and the inevitable questions that thereby arise; in view of the need for a properly theological assessment of the spirit of the times (such as of secularism, worldliness, subjectivism, humanism, the many varieties of atheism[24]—in view of all these things it is necessary that a team of theologians (and not the "court theologians") be at the disposal of the episcopacy, not merely to provide opinion on various *ad hoc* questions that may arise, but as a permanent advisory *gremium*. This is an excellent opportunity for intra-ecclesiastical dialogue, which might be realized as a sign of free, mutually respected *par cum pari*.

Of course, theology cannot, and does not, seek to replace the teaching authority of the Church, and has no intention of abrogating it. As a theology in and for the Church, it lives in the recognition and affirmation of the teaching authority. But it is also the case that the teaching authority cannot take the place of theological dialogue, for as Karl Rahner has recently pointed out, such dialogue is essential today as a means whereby the teaching authority prepares its own decisions and brings them to fruition. He then goes on to show that "up until very recent times, the teaching authority of the Church has not turned to the possibilities of assistance in theological dialogue in every appropriate or necessary case."[25] Such negligence can lead to erroneous or distorted decisions, and thus to difficulties. Rahner even puts it more directly as follows: "I think that many of the

[23] Cf. Chapter Seven, "Faith and Pluralism."
[24] Cf. Chapter Nine, "Faith and Atheism."
[25] K. Rahner, "Vom Dialog in der Kirche," in *Stimmen der Zeit* 179 (1967), pp. 81–95, especially p. 94.

promulgations of Pius XII would have had a different form and content if they had been preceded by an adequate, open, and free theological discussion of the corresponding questions. There is also no doubt that Paul VI turns a serious ear to theological debate as a preparation for authoritative decisions (or the decision not to decide, which can also be an important aspect of the teaching authority), even though, viewed from without, he thereby limits his own position. It can only be wished that the bishops will follow this example, for they also have a teaching authority, they also must put it to use, and they can defer to papal authority less today than in previous years. As in all concrete cases, dialogue between theologians and the teaching authority of the Church must come together in the unity of the process of finding and deepening the truth, so long as the dialogue persists, so long as it somehow terminates in an authoritative declaration, so long as the teaching authority must have the courage of silence as well as the courage of decision, insofar as all things cannot be deduced concretely from universal principles over and above the relationship between these two forces. We must always be searching for what is concrete in a decision, which ultimately cannot be accomplished theoretically, but actively, requiring at all times that we have the faith, the courage, the humility, and the will to accomplish the truth in love."[26]

[26] *Ibid.*, p. 94f.

CHAPTER FIVE

Faith and Hope

THE THOUGHTS that follow have to do with questions that have arisen in connection with the much discussed and very influential theology of hope. As a general introduction to this matter, we shall first take up several points of historical significance.

I

It is undeniably the case that historical movements and developments pass by today much more quickly than in the past. We have here one more indication of the intensity and pervasiveness of the phenomenon of historicity. Theology has also been influenced by this phenomenon. Theology has, in fact, been dominated by the rule of history to an even greater extent than the faith whose systematic reflection it seeks to become, because it is vitally moved by a concern to make use of the current possibilities and factors of human intellectual activity in the understanding of faith. Current developments in theology (especially Protestant theology, which has naturally tended to be more interested in what is new than in preserving continuity) give an indication of movement in that direction. In like manner, contemporary Catholic theology (in a sharp break with its past, which has chiefly been concerned with the continuity of tradition) has felt itself drawn by the force of this movement, insofar as it seeks to communicate with all theologians on the fundamental questions of theology as such, that is, insofar as it is marked by openness, not isolation; dialogue, not soliloquy. Although this particular characteristic of theology can be pointed to at each step and phrase of its development (it was, of course, not representative of theology as a whole, but was the mark of some of the greatest and most important theologians), it has become the distinctive trait and responsibility of the tasks of contemporary theology through the influence of the Second Vatican Council on the requirements of theology. The ecumenical theology proposed by the Council, signifying not a new area of study but a thorough restructuring of theology, cannot possibly be brought to realization without such openness, without contact with, and participation in, everything that in any way touches upon theology. That is the point of what will be sketched briefly in what follows.

In the interval between the end of the First and the end of the Second World War, Protestant theology[1] was heavily influenced by Karl Barth and his vast theological writings. Meanwhile (not completely, but through a clearly discernible change of accent), the influence of Rudolph Bultmann was also growing. Bultmann is a theologian who, together with Karl Barth and Emil Brunner, was the initiator of so-called dialectical theology and who then slowly but distinctly began to separate himself from Barth's "positivistic conception of revelation" (to use Dietrich Bonhoeffer's phrase) by means of existentialist theology, and to develop a different theological position. By his own admission, Karl Barth had this situation directly in mind in the final volumes of his *Church Dogmatics*, particularly in: *Rudolph Bultmann, ein Versich ihn zu verstehen.*[2] Here Barth takes the viewpoint (which culminates his theological critique) that Bultmann had fallen into the error the solution to which he had once tried to find, namely, the error of making existential pre-understanding the measure of the word of God. On his eightieth birthday Barth had warned about this theological position, particularly with regard to Catholic theologians, who, as he saw it, had allowed themselves to be influenced by Bultmann in too direct and uncritical a manner.

Nevertheless, for almost twenty years Bultmann, not Barth,

[1] Cf. H. Zahrnt, *Die Sache mit Gott* (Munich, 1966).

[2] (Zollikon–Zürich, 1952); cf. H. Fries, *Bultmann, Barth und die katholische Theologie* (Stuttgart, 1955).

reigned in Protestant theological circles. He became the most talked-about theologian in the world, stimulating a powerful movement lasting nearly a generation, and leaving his mark, both dogmatic and critical, on theological endeavors. He achieved this end through a thorough concentration and reduction of all theological statements to an existential interpretation. This approach lays out a theological program which accepts "everything that is written" and tries to draw out its inner meaning and deeper significance, thereby getting beyond what Bultmann considers to be an untenable, "positivistic conception of revelation." Existential interpretation becomes the key that opens every lock and door. It is impossible here to go into the full importance of this theology.[3]

Recently, however, it has been possible to discern the first clear indications of a *post-Bultmannian period*, a new movement with new aims and a different approach—a movement which, though it acknowledges its indebtedness to Bultmann (even where it disagrees with him most), is heading in a distinctly different direction.

This new phase in theology is characterized, on the one hand, by an extreme development of some of Bultmann's fundamental themes. This approach accepts the idea that theology is synonymous with anthropology, having as its prime concerns: what it means to be human; what it means to be human in association with others; and (in terms of the oughtness and obligation which pervade human being) the pressing problem of the "source of human abandonment."[4] It is a theology which, as one of its proponents has remarked, can no longer listen to the word "God," because it might turn out to be a "metaphysical idol." One position that has drawn considerable attention is Bonhoeffer's conception of a "religionless Christianity," which appears to be gaining strength insofar as (for example, in the

[3] H. Fries, "Entmythologisierung und theologische Wahrheit," in *Gott in Welt* I, pp. 366–391. For the purpose of orientation, cf. *Kerygma und Mythos*, edited by H. W. Bartsch, now at 6 vols. (Hamburg, 1948–1964).

[4] H. Braun, *Gesammelte Studien zum Neuen Testament und seiner Umwelt* (Tübingen, 1962), particularly pp. 243–309. Also H. Gollwitzer, *Die Existenz Gottes im Bekenntnis des Glaubens* (Munich[4], 1964).

United States) it is appealed to in defense of "death of God" theology.[5]

The post-Bultmannian era in theology is also characterized by the fact that some of his most famous disciples have rebelled against the master's position that one cannot, and should not, push beyond the biblical *kerygma* to a basis in historical occurrence and event. On the contrary, they admit and hold as theologically essential a much broader historical basis in the Bible, and particularly in the New Testament, than did Bultmann, who was of the opinion that besides the death of Christ there is nothing that can be attributed to the historical Jesus with any certainty. (Though it ought to be noted that Bultmann retracted some of his own earlier scepticism.) This position pervades Günter Bornkamm's well-known study of Jesus,[6] and scores of other works, particularly Ernst Käsemann's *Exegetischen Versuche und Besinnungen.*[7] It gains programmatic expression in the words attributed to Gerhard Ebeling: our faith in Christ has its support in the historical Jesus.[8]

Theology after Bultmann also regards the connection between formal historical method and existential theology as by no means necessary. Such a relationship was presupposed by Bultmann, who subordinated the formal historical method (which he helped establish and masterfully employed) to the existential mode of interpretation. The formal historical method, however, is compatible with, and strictly leads to, completely different conclusions. It calls for development in its own right.

A position clearly in opposition to Bultmann's is that which adopts as its theological orientation the idea of *revelation as history*,[9] and proposes therefore precisely what Bultmann rejects, namely, that revelation and biblical witness have to do with

[5] Cf. Chapter Nine, "Faith and Atheism."

[6] G. Bornkamm, *Jesus of Nazareth* (New York, 1960). A good overview of the whole problematic can be found in the anthology, *Der historische Jesus und der Christus des Glaubens*, edited by H. Ristow and K. Matthiae (Berlin², 1961); cf. J. R. Geiselmann, *Die Frage nach dem historischen Jesus* (Munich, 1965).

[7] Two volumes (Gottingen, 1965).

[8] G. Ebeling, *Theology and Proclamation* (New York, 1966), p. XYZ.

[9] Representative of this position is the work by W. Pannenberg, *Offen-*

events in history, with actual occurrences that are meaningful and revelatory in themselves and are irreducible to existential significance. In such a theological conception of "indirect revelation" Christ's resurrection from the dead, for example, is not taken to be a ground for belief in resurrection as such (for which there would be no basis in extra-subjective event), but is shown to signify the passage from fallenness and death to authenticity and freedom, operative in existence and perfected in word and faith. The resurrection is characterized as an event which simply cannot be taken as history, in the sense of existential correlation, analogy, and causality, but must be regarded as an occurrence and event in the sense of a new, non-analogous source that is realized and becomes operative in history.

Oscar Cullmann, the most representative and forceful advocate of the theology of the history of salvation, takes a different position by viewing time as a dimension proportionate to revelation, and history as the condition of possibility for revelation and salvation.[10] The history of salvation, for Cullmann, is the succession of events actuated and chosen by God. It is not at all identical with the continuum of historical occurrence, and is not bound mechanically to the empirico-historical series, but rather selects from this series certain special events and transforms them into instruments of revelation and salvation by means of a correlation between events and word. The direction of history towards salvation culminates in the person and actions of Jesus Christ, particularly in his resurrection from the dead. This theology can be contrasted with Bultmann's at several key junctures: insofar as it does not lay too great a stress on such alternatives as history over against historical sequence, or kerygma over against history; insofar as it grounds faith and witness in the "event of salvation" as its determination and actuation; and, in general, insofar as it strives to join together what Bultmann has

---

barung als Geschichte (Gottingen², 1963). Cf. also W. Pannenberg, *Grundzüge der Christologie* (Gutersloh², 1966).

[10] O. Cullmann, *Christ and Time* (Westminster, 1964); *Christology of the New Testament* (Westminster, 1964), and *Salvation as History* (New York, 1967).

separated. In distinction from Bultmann, for whom only the "now" of the presence of Christ, of witness, and of faith, can be significant and relevant, Cullmann works out a temporal determination of revelation in which all *tempora* have their determination. Cullmann characterizes the culminating revelation, fulfilled in Christ, as the "fullness of time," as expressed in the simple but significant ordinary use of the designations "before" and "after Christ." It appears specifically in the "already" of the decisive fulfillment given in Christ and the Christ-event, and in the "not yet" of the ultimate and inevitable majesty of the structure of revelation, of the future—the future of Jesus Christ, but a future that has already begun.

Perhaps the most striking development in post-Bultmannian theology is that which, if we accept its representation of the time-dimensionality of revelation as a starting point, characteristic, and criterion, makes the *tempus* of the *futurus* the decisive time of revelation. This conception, opposed to both the exclusivity of the "now" in Bultmann's theology and the exactitude of Cullmann's "already" and "not yet," declares that the very *nature of theology signifies hope*, and that hope implies the future as its one, proportionate time-determination. The future, which is described in the New Testament as that which is coming and is guaranteed with apocalyptic conceptions and categories, belongs, according to Bultmann, to the realm of unrealizable myth, the impossible, to what is beyond the expectations of present-day man. Biblical statements concerning judgment and resurrection, a "new heaven and a new earth," the fulfillment of the glory of God, can and must, according to Bultmann, be demythologized, given an existential interpretation, and made into a meaningful disclosure for, and only for, the present (strictly in line with the writings of John, which, according to Bultmann, have transposed the future into the present and declare: "Now is the judgment of the world" [John 12: 31]). Eschatological statements in the Bible and eschatological declarations of faith have nothing to do with some sort of "end" that is awaited in fear. Eschatological matters have exclusively to do with the "now" of the present moment.

In distinction from and opposition to this viewpoint, the theology of hope (whose best known representative today is Jürgen Moltmann[11]) places the future-oriented Christian eschatology at the center of the focus of theology. The biblical *futurus* is accepted as an ultimate criterion with complete seriousness and without any attempt to explain it away by means of the *praesens*. According to Moltmann, there is "only one real problem in Christian theology, which its own object forces upon it and which it in turn forces on mankind and on human thought: the problem of the future" (p. 16). The future, the hope in something to come as a reality, an event, a state of affairs, is the theme of a theology which, on the basis of this principle (and principle here indicates both origin and control), is capable of comprehending all things and bringing them to clear understanding (something which must also be said, at least formally, of Bultmann's principle).

We have some idea of how thoroughly and completely Moltmann views hope as the principle of theology by noting that he transforms the scholastic phrase "*fides quaerens intellectum*" into "*spes quaerens intellectum,*" and also absorbs the phrase "*credo, ut intelligam*" into "*spero, ut intelligam*" (p. 36). From this vantage point, theology becomes *docta spes*. Moltmann explains this transformation in the following passage: ". . . it could well be that it is of decisive importance for Christian theology today to follow the basic principle: *spes quaerens intellectum—spero, ut intelligam*. If it is hope that maintains and upholds faith and keeps it moving on, if it is hope that draws the believer into the life of love, then it will also be hope that is the mobilizing and driving force of faith's thinking, of its knowledge of, and reflections on, human nature, history, and society. Faith hopes in order to know what it believes" (p. 33).

[11] J. Moltmann, *Theology of Hope*; "Die Kategorie Novum in der christlichen Theologie," in *Ernst Bloch zu ehren*, edited by S. Unseld (Frankfurt, 1965), pp. 243–255; "Der Realismus der Hoffnung," in *Kontexte* I (Stuttgart–Berlin, 1966), pp. 101–107; *Diskussion über die "Theologie der Hoffnung" von Jürgen Moltmann*, edited by W.-D. Marsch (Munich, 1967). References are to page numbers in the English translation.

Of course, the theology of hope establishes an essential and necessary correlation with *faith.* Moltmann devotes a thorough reflection on this correlation. Hope is faith unfolded. "Faith binds man to Christ. Hope sets this faith open to the comprehensive future of Christ. . . . Thus in the Christian life faith has the priority, but hope the primacy. Without faith's knowledge of Christ, hope becomes a utopia and remains hanging in the air. But without hope, faith falls to pieces, becomes a faint-hearted and ultimately a dead faith. It is through faith that man finds the path of true life, but it is only hope that keeps him on that path. Thus it is that faith in Christ gives hope its assurance. Thus it is that hope gives faith in Christ its breadth and leads it to life" (p. 20).

Hope is all the more convincing as the principle of theology when, in the words of the Second Vatican Council, it is grounded in the "focus and fullness of the whole of revelation," that is, in Jesus Christ and his resurrection from the dead, which encompasses all the other events of salvation. "Christianity stands or falls with the reality of the raising of Jesus from the dead by God. . . . A Christian faith that is not a resurrection faith can be called neither Christian nor faith" (p. 166).

Because the Easter events are the ground for hope, an interpretation of the resurrection of Christ has a central role in Moltmann's theology of hope. Moltmann sharply contrasts his understanding of this event with an existential interpretation, stating that the event of Easter is not an "expression of" but an "explanatory statement"; that the word which bears witness does not mean "I am certain," but "it is certain." In their historical considerations Bultmann and many of his disciples objected to regarding the resurrection of Christ as an event or occurrence; these same considerations are taken by Moltmann to indicate that Easter, as an absolute, new, and future-oriented beginning, must be described (along with several other events) as a common category immanent to the world. No argument can be posed against Easter from the historical "experience" of the world; rather, from the vantage point of the Easter event, experience must be newly understood and revised. This vantage point, this ever-present "Copernican" revolution in Christian theology, is something which Karl Barth constantly referred to in his opposition to Bultmann. The resurrection of Christ is analogous not to something that is constantly being experienced, but to something that is yet to come to everyone (p. 163). The resurrection is historical because, "by pointing the way for future events, it *makes* history in which we can and must live insofar as it points the way to a future event. It is historic, because it discloses an eschatological future" (p. 181). The Easter event has only *one* analogy disclosed by faith: the creation of the world from nothing. The Epistle to the Romans (4: 17) speaks of the God who raises the dead and calls non-being into being (p. 25).

However, according to Moltmann the Easter event also stands squarely in the horizon of promise: the future in Jesus Christ, the new creation, the resurrection of all men from the dead, the universal glory of God, the fact "that God [will be] all in all" (1 Corinthians 15: 28). This future, which is not to be the "reappearance of what has gone before," but the advent of what is now immanent, has become the "object of hope" through the resurrection of him who was crucified: "Christ is the first-fruit of those who have fallen asleep" (1 Corinthians 15: 20). Those who lay claim to Christ, according to Moltmann, should not be so concerned with describing who Christ was, as with laboring to understand who he will be. The situation of the world, and man's destiny in the world, are interpreted in terms of the Easter event understood as promise—not, with Kierkegaard, as the paradoxical presence of the eternal in the existential "now," but as the "eschatological difference" given in the anticipation of what is to come. What is to come becomes transparent in the manifold negative experiences of the present in history.

The Easter event itself, however, according to Moltmann, is to be taken neither as the reception of the mortal and crucified Christ in the presence of those who have been raised from the dead, nor simply as a sign of the significance of the cross (a significance for which Easter is not an event *including* Christ, but the birth of faith in the witness of Christ), nor as the identity of the crucified and resurrected Christ in the person of Jesus.

The identity of the crucified and resurrected Christ given in Easter is to be found, according to Moltmann, "in the God who creates life and new being out of nothing. He is then wholly dead and wholly raised" (p. 200). Once again, the Easter event clearly is a promise. It is an event in which God confesses to God and reveals his faithfulness. It points back to the promises of God and forwards to "an *eschaton* in which his divinity is revealed in all."

The ever-present problem concerning the difference between the historical Jesus and the Christ of faith is given a penetrating answer from this vantage point: here there are no discrepancies, but rather a necessary correspondence that is conditioned, and even required, by the resurrection of Christ. Albert Schweitzer's statement that "Christ proclaimed the kingdom, and the Church proclaimed—him" is no longer a contradiction, but rather articulates a fundamental, biblical truth: the concrete form of the kingdom of God as the dominion of God over death, as manifested in the Easter event (p. 219).

A theology of hope so conceived leads to certain implications and consequences, and Moltmann has clearly seen them. If hope, along with its presupposition, *promise*, is made the principle of theology, then revelation and revelational events cannot be understood as an epiphany, that is, as self-manifestation, as the exposition of *doxa*, as the "dis-closure" of the hidden God. These latter positions introduce categories and horizons under which the events of revelation, as recounted in the Bible, are in danger of being subsumed into terms whereby the Greek religion becomes the measure of biblical witness. The incontestable dominance of the Old Testament testimony that God reveals himself by means of promises and in the history of such promises, becomes, for Moltmann, the determining horizon for biblical revelation as such, and for the decisive position of Old Testament events in the history of salvation as the guide for an understanding of Christ (p. 149). "The examination in the field of comparative religion of the special peculiarity of Israelite faith is today bringing out ever more strongly the difference between its 'religion of promise' and the epiphany religions of the revealed gods of the world around Israel. These epiphany religions are all 'religions of revelation' in their own way. Any place in the world can become the epiphany of the divine and the pictorial transparency of the deity. The essential difference here is accordingly not between the so-called nature gods and a God of revelation, but between the God of the promise and the gods of the epiphanies. Thus the difference does not lie already in the assertion of divine 'revelation' as such, but in the different ways of conceiving and speaking of the revelation and self-manifestation of the deity. The decisively important question is obviously that of the context in which the talk of revelation arises. It is one thing to ask: where and when does an epiphany of the divine, eternal, immutable, and primordial take place in the realm of the human, temporal, and transient? And it is another thing to ask: when and where does the God of the promise reveal his faithfulness and in it himself and his presence? The one question asks about the presence of the eternal, the other about the future of what is promised. But if promise is determinative of what is said of the revealing of God, then every theological view of biblical revelation contains implicitly a governing view of eschatology" (p. 43).

This theological conception has a correlate and corresponding expression in theological language. The epiphany of God is related to the *logos*, which manifests and bears witness to what is, the very essence of things; which reveals the truth about the existence of whatever is; which sees in the *logos* the epiphany the eternal present of being, and therein finds truth (p. 40); which can draw this truth into the form of systematic doctrine. The problematic certainty of eschatology as "doctrine" is measured by its relation to reality, "which is there, now and always, and is given true expression in the word and is brought to truth by means of an accurate representation in language appropriate to it. In this sense, there can be no *logos* of the future" (p. 17). Consequently, the proper theological mode of language should be such that "in the medium of hope our theological concepts become not judgments which nail reality down to what it is, but anticipations which show reality its prospects and its future possibilities. Theological concepts do not give a fixed form to reality, but they are expanded by hope and anticipate future being. They do not limp after reality and gaze on it with the night-eyes of Minerva's owl, but they illuminate reality displaying its future. Their knowledge is grounded not in the will to dominate, but in love to the future of things ... They are thus concepts which are engaged in a process of movement, conceived in action and which call forth practical movement and change" (pp. 35–36).

The differentiation of Greek from Judeo-Christian thought, of *logos* from promise, of epiphany from apocalypse of truth—a differentiation fundamental to both the Old and the New Testament—is a never-ending task that today especially must be given careful attention and consideration. "Christian eschatology in the language of promise will then be an essential key to the unlocking of Christian truth. For the loss of eschatology—not merely as an appendix to dogmatics, but as the medium of theological thinking as such—has always been the condition that makes possible the adaptation of Christianity to its environment and, as a result of this, the self-surrender of faith. Just as in theological thought the blending of Christianity with the Greek mind made it no longer clear which God was really being spoken of, so Christianity in its social form took over the heritage of the ancient state religion. It installed itself as the 'crown of society' and its 'saving centre', and lost the disquieting, critical power of its eschatological hope. In place of what the Epistle to the Hebrews describes as an exodus from the fixed camp and the continuing city, there came the solemn entry into society of a religious transfiguration of the world" (pp. 41–42).

On the basis of this premiss the "theology of hope" pits itself against the "enthusiasm of fulfillment," already to be found in early Christianity, which, according to Moltmann, came about through the influence of Greek epiphanic piety. This sort of piety is completely foreign to eschatological expectation and hope. It lives in the present fulfillment of the epiphany of God, which the Christ event posits as the eschatological presence of eternity. Eternity is one with ultimacy, and ultimacy is bound up with the end of time (p. 157). The fact of promise becomes the process of redemption, a process that is celebrated in worship. "The resurrection of Jesus is regarded as his exaltation and enthronement and is related to his incarnation. To be sure, his humiliation even to the cross can be understood as the perfecting of his incarnation, by means of which he draws all things into the sphere of his lordship, yet the cross is in this way made only a transitional stage on his way to heavenly lordship. The cross does not remain until the fulfilment of the *eschaton* the abiding key-signature of his lordship in the world. If his resurrection is understood in this sense as his heavenly enthronement, then the sacramental event which represents him in the cultus becomes a parallel to his incarnation and is taken as an earthly adumbration and accomplishment of his heavenly lordship, his heavenly life in the realm of the things that are earthly, transient and split up into a multitude of forces. History thus loses its eschatological direction. It is not the realm in which men suffer and hope, groaning and travailing in expectation of Christ's future for the world, but it becomes the field in which the heavenly lordship of Christ is disclosed in Church and sacrament. In place of the eschatological 'not yet' [*noch nicht*] we have a cultic 'not only' [*nur noch*], and this becomes the key-signature of history *post Christum*" (pp. 158–159).

With regard to such positions, it must be said that the principle of hope loses sight of its origin and power. If history *post Christum* is understood in this way, it can only be taken as a misunderstanding of what is the true source.

If Moltmann were to reflect on the *Church*, he could not take it to be an institution functioning for the *cultus publicus*, nor could it be characterized as a "life principle of human society." Its position and existence establish it as an exodus community, as the wandering people of God, who wander in the horizon of expectation of the kingdom of God. The mission of the Church, in a situation pervaded by despondency, despair, hopelessness, and doubt—these, not *hybris*, are the original sins—is to fill the world with Christian hope and extend it everywhere. The task of the Church is "to inject this hope into mankind."

Further, the existence of the Church thereby also becomes a peculiarly active and creative force. It will not bend under the "normative power of the facts." It will not passively and submissively let things run their course; it will not compromise with them, nor sublimate them into a misconstrued, ideologically tarnished faith. It accepts the world, and above all the men who live in the world, as they are. It will do everything in its power in order to lead the world into this future, and to prepare it for the dominion of God. It will recognize the responsibility that accompanies this motivation, a responsibility that extends to all things—the world and mankind—and will do everything it can in order to become engaged in the righteousness and freedom of the world. In the midst of sickness, suffering, poverty, and death, it will not simply recognize what has been decreed, and what is allowed, but, in conformity with the biblical mandate, it will seek out the "enemies" (see 1 Corinthians 15: 25) in order to do battle with them and to conquer them. It will not be merely concerned with healing wounds, but with doing everything it can in order to prevent such wounds.

All in all, a theology of hope accomplishes a number of things. It succeeds in a real determination and characterization of Christianity. To be a Christian means to have hope. Christians are distinguished from those "who have no hope" (1 Thessalonians 4: 13). Therefore, Christians must "develop their understanding of faith, in all of its ramifications, as eschatology. Eschatology, in a Christian theology, cannot be taken merely as a local matter. It must be radically accepted as the form of every theological statement."[12] Theology of hope arrives at an intensive concentration of Christianity and what follows from it for the individual and for the Church. It succeeds in overthrowing a perspective of faith that is restricted to the past and the present, a perspective that can lead to reassurance, complacency, self-contentment, and passivity. Hope which transcends and engages is a constant element of the dynamism present in and required by the Christian faith. This hope is a spur to action, to assistance,

[12] J. B. Metz, "Verantwortung der Hoffnung," in *Stimmen der Zeit* 177 (1966), p. 457.

to solidarity with the world, without becoming identified with the world. It recognizes its function as a constant preparedness for service and assistance.

Theology of hope also overcomes the difficulties that attend the various notions, categories, and vocabulary of faith and theology that stem from an ancient, mythological conception of the world, and it does this by substituting the *future* for the category of the hereafter, of transcendence. The "God above us" becomes the "God out in front of us"—the God of promise, the God of the future. This viewpoint does away with those conceptions and attitudes of faith that would have "God behind us," in back of us.

Theology of hope, in a very unique manner, has immediate significance insofar as it gives direction to man's anticipation of the future—not merely of one's own private future, but of the entire future of us all. It is oriented to the future of man, and attempts to give it accurate expression, and take into account the consequences and responsibility of the hope that fills Christian life (see 1 Peter 3: 15).

Hope has been given too little attention in Christian faith, and it has rarely been transformed into action. Further, it has been limited to the private sphere (and its direct issue into expectation and the shaping of the future of man and his world). All this has led to failure and created a void that has now been filled by a secularized *principle of hope* (particularly in Ernst Bloch), and especially by the future-directed energy and dynamism that is found in Marxism. The only possible answer to this situation and its "challenge" (see Toynbee) is found in a theology of hope.[13]

II

In line with what has been said so far, it should be clear that this wide-ranging and impressive theology of hope, especially in

[13] In the most recent edition of his book, J. Moltmann has taken up a discussion of E. Bloch's *Prinzip der Hoffnung*. Cf. also J. Moltmann, "Das 'Prinzip Hoffnung' und die christliche Zubersicht: Ein Gespräch

its fundamental position, *spero, ut intelligam*, is a matter of deep significance.

At the level of action, hope can be taken to be a defining characteristic of what life, faith, and existence in Christ means. According to 1 Peter 3: 15, the task of the Christian is described as the readiness to give an account of and an answer to the "hope that is in you." Hope is an extension of faith. It describes the future-oriented aspect of faith.[14] The gospel can be taken to be the gospel of hope.[15] To distinguish the Christian from among the rest is to distinguish one who has hope from those "who have no hope." The classic characterization of faith in the Epistle to the Hebrews (11: 1) makes clear the connection and correlation between faith and hope: "Faith is the substance of things to be hoped for."

Furthermore, hope gives unmistakable expression to the state of the Christian and the Church, namely, the role of the pilgrimage, the wandering people of God, who know what the end of their journey is, but do not forget that they have not yet attained it.[16]

On the basis of what has been said so far, it is perfectly valid to make hope the principle of theology, and to work out a theology by means of that principle. But it must also be made clear that theology of hope is radically grounded in Jesus Christ, in his person and in his life. It is eminently Christian insofar as the hope of glory is "Christ in you" (Colossians 1: 27), that is, insofar as the central event and message of the New Testament, the paschal mystery, the crucifixion, and resurrection of Christ,

---

mit Ernst Bloch," in *EvTh* 23 (1963), pp. 537–557; and "Hope over Belief?" in *Concilium* 2 (Glen Rock, 1962).

[14] O. Kuss, *Der Römerbrief: Erste Lieferung* (Regensburg, 1957), pp. 195–198; P. Hoffmann, "Hoffnung," in *HthG* I (Munich, 1962), pp. 698–702.

[15] R. Bultmann, *Theologie des Neun Testaments*[3] (Tübingen, 1953), pp. 127f.; K. H. Rengstorf and R. Bultmann, "ἐλπίς," in *ThWNT* II (Stuttgart, 1935), pp. 515–531.

[16] Cf. H. Schlier, "On Hope," in *The Relevance of the New Testament* (New York, 1968), pp. 142–155; J. Pieper, *Uber die Hoffnung* (Munich, 1961), and "Hoffnung," in *HthG* I, pp. 702–706, and *Hoffnung und Geschichte* (Munich, 1967).

are viewed as the source and ground of this hope. The future that we wait and hope for is the future in Jesus Christ, or more precisely the future that has been opened to all men through his resurrection from the dead, the future of life as conquest over death, as the absolutely inevitable coming of the kingly glory of God. In light of all this, the fact that theology of hope refuses to accept as obvious the modern criteria of what constitutes an historical event, and from this point to specify what is "possible" and "impossible" as an instance of revelation, is not sufficiently appreciated, for it is due to this position that the future is understood not as the confirmation of a present-oriented and existentially based interpretation of eschatology, but as the indication of an approaching event which we must wait and hope for.

Theology of hope acquires its theological qualifications and legitimacy by taking, so to speak, the whole into its perspective, by excluding nothing, by maintaining the focal point within the whole, and consequently, in line with the Second Vatican Council, by showing concern for the *hierarchia veritatum.*

Theology of hope takes on particular significance in light of the fact that the theme of hope has always been a neglected object of theological concern and reflection. Theology has occupied itself too exclusively with the themes of faith (above all, faith) and love. The subject of hope was one among others. It was usually taken up, and then only cursorily, with regard to the three "divine virtues." But no attempt had ever been made to make hope the principle of theology. The theology of hope that we have been considering is capable of lifting hope from the sphere of the private and the individual, and, without diminishing the personal element, elevating it to the dimension of the community, the Church, humanity. It is only in this way that hope attains its true, universal aspect.[17] Theology of hope then shows the possibility of providing an answer to the question posed by contemporary man, who is troubled by nothing so much as the question of the future.

[17] Cf. M. Schmaus, *Katholische Dogmatik* IV/2: *Die Lehre von den letzten Dingen* (Munich, 1959); H. Schlier, "Das, worauf alles wartet," in *Interpretation der Welt*, edited by H. Kuhn, H. Kahlefeld, and K. Forster (Wurzburg, 1965), pp. 599–616.

We have already indicated that theology of hope is in an ideal position to enter into dialogue with the most clearly defined contemporary world-view, namely, Marxism, and also that a theology of "God out in front of us" helps overcome the difficulties that plague contemporary man caught up in a theology of "God above us."[18]

Finally, with particular reference to the Catholic mind, a theology of hope, or hope understood as the principle of theology, makes it clear that the Church, the community of those who hope, must be filled with life, trust, and true youthfulness, that it must neither be drawn in and paralyzed by the history of the past, by the single aim of justifying antiquity, nor completely spent and exhausted in the present. Hope is capable of keeping the Church constantly aware of the fact that it is in process, that it cannot identify itself with the kingdom of God or anticipate its glory, but that it is incomplete, *ecclesia semper reformanda*, capable of, and in need of, renewal.

III

The following critical remarks are to be taken only under the explicit premiss of the positive evaluation and assessment that has preceded. They are primarily directed to the ideas of Moltmann and have less the flavor of assertions than questions. Further, these critical questions are related not so much to what Moltmann has said, as to what he has not said, or to what has been given alternative consideration.

First of all, in Moltmann's theology of hope, promise is separated from the declaration given in the *logos* as well as from the commentary presented through kerygma, because promise is separated, as a category of Christian revelation, from epiphany. But it is invalid to approach this point by means of alternatives, because that would lead to one-sidedness. Likewise, it is by no means necessary to pose such alternatives from the viewpoint of hope.

[18] Cf. J. B. Metz, "Gott vor uns," in *Ernst Bloch zu ehren*, pp. 227–241; and "Verantwortung der Hoffnung," in *Stimmen der Zeit* 177 (1966), pp. 451–462.

It cannot be denied (and Moltmann does not) that revelation in the New Testament is presented as a fulfillment, in the sense of a decision that is to be made today, now. This insight is one of the lasting contributions of Bultmann's theology. It persists even though it became so one-sided that Bultmann finally denied that there is a real future, in the sense of an event, an occurrence, for which we are still waiting. Bultmann's theology of the present, of decision, cannot be resolved by a radically posed theology of the future, of hope. That would be to replace one form of one-sidedness with another. It can only be resolved by a theological understanding that considers the present and the future together, that views the present as the beginning of the future and the future as the self-fulfillment of the present. Of course, it is true that the conjunction of the present and the future, the already-has-been and the still-to-come, is not characteristic of the New Testament. However, if we stop to consider where the accent is, not only in the sense of priority but of primacy, we find that it is on the now, on today. Because something happened, something else, not yet here, will happen. What is to happen is the self-realization of what has already happened —its development, its universal extension and expansion. It is because we believe in the present-at-hand, because it is a part of the existential order, that we can hope for the future.

In distinction from Bultmann, it is also in line with the New Testament to speak of a fulfillment, an *ecce*, given in the life and person of Jesus Christ,[19] that is, an epiphany present in Jesus Christ—a sense of presence which has to do not only with hearing, but with seeing: "We have seen his glory" (John 1: 14). This sort of revelation cannot be adequately and sufficiently described solely by means of the category of promise.

Moltmann denies that New Testament revelation, culminating in the Christ event, in Jesus Christ, can be understood on the basis of epiphany, a viewpoint which finds expression in the notions of worship and sacrament. Moltmann traces the corresponding statements in the New Testament to the influence of Greek religions, especially the mystery religions, which were

[19] Cf. H. Fries, *Revelation*; H. Urs von Balthasar, *Herrlichkeit* I.

characterized by *logos* and epiphany. But these statements, if we push Moltmann's interpretations a bit farther, although they are only required as instruments of interpretation, do not correspond to the true source of New Testament witness.

It is more fundamental to ask whether or not an interpretation of revelation in Christ by means of the categories of epiphany and *logos* is legitimate. It is only by means of these categories that the ultimacy, the final word, "the Word that was made flesh and dwelt among us," the fullness and the fulfillment, can be given a legitimate expression. Without them, these things cannot be given a completely adequate representation. It has nothing to do with a fixation on fulfillment or with an insistence on the "now only," but with the knowledge that the New Testament represents a phase and dimension entirely different from those of the Old Testament; that what has been promised has come, that "we need wait for no other" (see Matthew 11: 3); that God has made and fulfilled in him all true promises; that he is the great, unlimited, unrepeatable "Yes" (see 2 Corinthians 1: 20); that Jesus *is* the Christ, the *Kyrios*, and that the Christian stance is precisely to articulate this presence in an unlimited variety of ways.

In principle, these facts are not at all excluded from theology of hope. What we are concerned about in these remarks has to do with the proper accent and the right proportions, the manner in which the whole is brought to fruition.

From this point of view we can no more abandon the statement which expresses the epiphany, or the preaching kerygma related to the here and now, than we can ignore promise as expressing the future in Jesus Christ, for only together do they measure to the whole that is given witness in the New Testament.

With regard to the consideration of the influence of the Greek frame of mind as an element foreign to biblical categories, it must be said that the oft-cited unequivocality and exclusivity of biblical thought and language simply do not hold. The presence of Greek thought in the New Testament, and in the theology that it contains, is a valid and legitimate circumstance. Only in this way can the revelation, epiphany, and promise fulfilled in

Jesus Christ be for all people—or, as we find it in the Bible, "for Jews and Gentiles." As a consequence, if the messenger of the truth of the gospel, the witness of Jesus as Christ and *Kyrios*, is to be all things to all people—a Jew to the Jews, a Greek to the Greeks (see 1 Corinthians 9: 20)—then the elements of Greek thought—*logos*, epiphany, presence—cannot be excluded. They must be admitted, and are even required, in order to articulate that to which the New Testament gives witness. What appears to be an extraneous influence turns out to be, upon closer examination, the realization of universality, an expansion in all directions.

Consequently, it is not a matter of denying the category of promise, and the corresponding reality of hope, in the New Testament, but rather denying that such exclusive alternatives are required to represent this principle. It is a matter of emphasizing that the theology of hope is in a position to develop its true position, its ground, and the power of its efficacy, not through the exclusion of, but through correlation with, the whole, including the truth of *logos*, of epiphany, notification, statement, commentary, and promise.

It is in this whole that we find the whole of "already" and "not yet." If, however, it should be asked where the priority and primacy lie, then the answer has to be: in what has "already" happened.

If it is absolutely correct to say that hope is faith as it is developed, this characterization must be expanded by saying that hope develops faith in a specific dimension, namely, in the dimension of the future. However, this dimension is not the whole of faith itself. Faith also has its development with regard to the past, i.e., namely, into its origins (especially with regard to the present), in which it not only brings itself, but the present that is given in itself, to realization. Consequently, it must be said that *faith is the comprehensive and inclusive principle of theology*. It is possible—and completely possible—to develop hope in terms of faith, but hope is not the only horizon in which faith can be described. It is impossible to conjugate and spell the *credo*, and all that it contains, simply in terms of the future. Faith is related to the whole, which includes hope. According to

Hebrews 11: 1, faith is the "support of hope." It is, therefore, its source as well as the measure of its truth.[20] As a consequence, faith not only has priority, but primacy. *Credo, ut intelligam* has priority and primacy over *spero, ut intelligam.*

Spero, ut intelligam is certainly in the position to describe the basic, undivided source of the history of salvation, and the relationship between the Old and New Testaments. But at the same time, there is the danger that, through the category of hope and promise alone, the difference between the old and the new covenant (which can be defined basically as the difference between promise and fulfillment, where fulfillment becomes the ground of new promise) cannot be clearly enough defined. The Jesus event is not only an act of promise, but, despite Moltmann's doubts about it (p. 156), an act of salvation, which must be characterized in the indicative mood as the blessing, justification, and salvation of man in the present.

Moltmann's claim that the Old Testament experience can be taken as a guide for the Christ event (p. 148) is extremely important, but it loses this importance when it is made into an exclusive principle. We can hardly afford to overlook the decisive fact that only by means of the (incomparably) New Testament, the completely different Christ event, can the Old Testament revelation be placed in its proper role in the history of salvation, and accurately assessed in terms of its true importance. In any event, that is how the New Testament itself was conceived, written, and regarded. Augustine's famous statement, "*In Vetere Testamento Novum Testamentum latet, in Novo Testamento Vetus Testamentum patet,*" still has its value today as a hermeneutical principle. Certainly, what has gone before gives some kind of pre-knowledge of the end. But the end brings ultimate knowledge, and that, as something new, can mean a complete correction of the pre-knowledge based on what has gone before. Here we must ask whether a theology of hope, so conceived, can sufficiently explain the definiteness, the ultimacy of the revelation present in Christ; whether it devotes sufficient attention to the past and the present, to the true significance of

[20] H. Schlier, "On Hope," p. 148.

the here and now as present in the word and the sacraments (which are totally absorbed in being the cause and ground of hope); and thus whether it gives adequate expression to the salvation operative in the here and now.

Although Moltmann's theology, with good grounds, attempts to indicate involvement in the present on the basis of hope, and to frame the imperativeness of solidarity, love, and brotherhood, it still must be asked if the future is the essence of faith and the focus of Christian existence. Is it not also possible that, for the sake of the future, we might flee from the present, or take a disinterest in it? Are not the incontestable demands and appeals proposed by Moltmann more meaningful when understood in the indicative mood? For example: "Become what you are," "Have this mind in you which was also in Christ Jesus" (Philippians 2: 5), or the command and authorization of Jesus Christ to go the way of Jesus in love for mankind, in existence for others. A foundation in the principle "Become what you will be" (p. 147) is not impossible, but it is not incapable of giving expression to every impulse and motive.

The theological principle of hope has also become the basis for the development of a distinctively active and involved political theology which neither seeks merely to understand and clarify, nor to lead in such a way as merely to justify itself in the existential order, or to pass judgment, or to endure, or to suffer, but rather, impelled by this hope, it seeks to change the world in the sign of hope, to struggle against needs and wants of every form and dimension, to make the world ever more a human world, a down-to-earth world of freedom, righteousness, and happiness, in order to prepare the world for the coming of the glory of God. However, a question remains (without at all taking away one jot from these demanding, but sorely neglected duties), namely: Does not this approach possibly take the future of the glory of God away from dependency on God and place it in the hands of mankind? Does the way of hope become identified with evolution? Is not the New Testament an ultimate testimony on behalf of the fact that the kingdom of God can neither be built nor made, that we can ask only for its coming, realizing that a preparation for it is putting the matter completely and radically backwards? We must ask, further, if a world that has been changed and improved, and where the struggle goes on against suffering and death, is the specific object of New Testament hope? Josef Pieper has put the question correctly when he asks wherein lies the hope of the martyrs, that is, "those for whom expectations for something in the world, for whom simple survival in the struggle for the realization of reighteousness, have become utterly nothing; those who find themselves, by contrast, in an utterly hopeless situation—in the death cell, in a concentration camp, without rights, morbidly ridiculous, abandoned, given over to the scorn of the privileged." Pieper closes these reflections with the statement: "Let us rather be silent about hope when there is none for the martyrs."[21] Finally, we must ask whether the Bible does not present us with a different picture of the advance of history on the face of the earth, namely, that "heaven and earth will pass away" (Matthew 24: 35)—and the more so as we move into the future, whose advent is the object of all hope?

It is, without doubt, a real theological problem to consider the extent to which hopes that are realized in the world, and the transformations of the world that they occasion, can be integrated into the believing hope for "the citizenship in heaven" (Philippians 3: 20), for the "new heaven and new earth" (Revelation 21: 1), and the "new Jerusalem." The answer works itself out necessarily, and dialectically, between the "no" of a theological dualism and the "yes" grounded in the history of salvation and its optimism with regard to progress.[22]

The fact that the Church is the wandering people of God, and that it lives in the proclamation of its true preparatoriness for, and its "historical, progressive absorption into, the kingdom of God, towards which it moves in pilgrimage in order to reach it,"[23] has been clarified with regard to the Catholic understand-

[21] J. Pieper, *Hoffnung und Geschichte*, p. 40.

[22] P. Engelhardt, "Hoffnung," in *LThK*² 5 (1960), pp. 422–424.

[23] K. Rahner, "Kirche und Parusie Christi," in *Schriften zur Theologie* VI, p. 351.

ing of the Church by the Second Vatican Council in its *Dogmatic Constitution on the Church.* However, this statement must remain united with that other truth, that in the Church, through its service in word and sacraments, the salvation that has come in the Christ event is made present and communicated, that the fullness and richness of Christ are developed in time and in the world, and that the modernization that it has been charged with succeeds basically through its faithfulness to its origin.

What is under consideration at present can be understood in the fact that Moltmann distinguishes the category of modernization in Christian theology from the kind of *re-novare* that has to do with a reinstitution of antiquity, namely, *restitutio in integrum.* However, it is unmistakable that the modernization attributed to Christian hope, amidst all that is new, is a renewal oriented in Christ, that it stems from its origin as well as from its future, that it does not transcend the horizon opened through Jesus Christ. Thus the Church becomes new through renewal, whether it be an elementary or a gigantic movement forward.

From this point of view continuity is preserved, and this is an aspect of real history and historicity just as much as what is new, unexpected, and incalculable.

For an understanding of the "distinction of being Christian," it does not suffice to distinguish the so-called linear approach to time from the cyclical, and then to pose an alternative. It has to do, rather, with the quest for a synthesis and integration as required by the fact that source and goal, advent and origin, are coordinated in history,[24] although for the history of man, the identity of source and goal has not yet been realized. The biblical testimony for this fact are the words of Christ according to John (words that also apply to mankind): "I came forth from the Father and have come into the world. Again I leave the world and go to the Father" (John 16: 28).

In the sacraments, especially, the dimensions of origin, present, and future are strongly united. They are an *anamnesis,*

[24] Cf. M. Seckler, *Das Heil in der Geschichte* (Munich, 1964); H. Fries, "Die Zeit als Element der christlichen Offenbarung," in *Interpretation der Welt,* pp. 701–712; J. Pieper, "Herkunftslose Zukunft und Hoffnung ohne Grund?," in *Hochland* 59 (1967), pp. 575–582.

a reflective remembrance of what once happened and took place; they are a representation of this past occurrence with regard to its efficacy in the here and now; they are a sign of a future request and pledge. This point of view gained classic expression in the well-known words of Thomas of Aquin on the Eucharist, as a "*convivium, in quo Christus sumitur, recolitur memoria passionis eius, mens impletur gratia et futurae gloriae nobis pignus datur.*"

Certainly, theology of hope has been successful in turning away from that familiar other-worldliness and transcendence of God which, within the limits of a contemporary understanding of the world, is attended with so many difficulties; and it has opened our view to the future, to the "God out in front of us," and thus offers a unique horizon of understanding for contemporary man. And if theological efforts are being made to bring together what "for so long has been unhealthily separated in theology, namely, transcendence and future, in view of the future-orientation of the Christian faith demanded by the gospel itself,"[25] then such efforts, for the sake of the wholeness and fullness of the content of revelation, must be greeted with open arms. But we should not thereby lose sight of the fact that the future of the Christian faith, that Christian hope and what it affirms, that the "God out in front of us," will not seem less capable of belief from the viewpoint of contemporary man than the other-worldliness and transcendence of God, the "God above us." We may cite Bultmann's program of demythologization as an example in this regard, which, with reference to the scientific view of the world and the philosophic self-understanding of modern man, not only demythologized the world-view that we find in the Bible and the theological statements constructed from its elements, but also the future-oriented declarations of the New Testament, which Bultmann took as a mythic eschatology that "is eliminated basically by the simple fact that the *parousia* of Christ did not take place as the New Testament had expected, but that the world went on its course, and, as everyone in his

[25] J. B. Metz, "Verantwortung der Hoffnung," in *Stimmen der Zeit* 177 (1966), p. 453.

right mind is convinced, will continue to go on its course."[26] This point is not an argument against the theology of hope, but it can, perhaps, keep us from attaching to it any false or exaggerated expectations. Heinz Zahrnt characterizes the situation this way: "The vertical has become stretched into the horizontal. Once it was the case that man sought to flee 'upwards' from the crash of reality, but today he flees 'forwards.' But whether the flight now is upwards, or forwards, in both cases the proof for the truth of God (spatially or temporally) is placed in some indeterminate distance."[27]

These remarks would be entirely misunderstood if they were to be taken as an attempt to cast suspicion upon theology of hope—as false, or inadequate—or to declare it as a wholly deficient theology. They neither seek, nor are they capable, of doing that. No less do they seek to withdraw the positive and appreciative attitude expressed at the beginning of the chapter, or to minimize it through a critique of trivialities. These critical remarks have no other meaning than to affirm and support that theology. This end seems possible only by freeing it from arbitrary alternatives and possible one-sidedness, which perhaps could make its acceptance more difficult, and to integrate it into the greater measure of the whole—*spero, ut intelligam* into *credo, ut intelligam*, hope into faith.[28]

[26] R. Bultmann, "New Testament and Mythology," in *Kerygma and Myth* I.

[27] H. Zahrnt, *Die Sache mit Gott*, p. 259.

[28] For the current state of the question, cf. *Diskussion über die "Theologie der Hoffnung,"* edited by W.-D. Marsch (Munich, 1967). In this work, J. Moltmann gives a detailed response to criticism of the theology of hope (pp. 201–238).

CHAPTER SIX

Faith and Ideology

I

ANY LEXICON, as well as our own rather careless use of language, can instruct us on the various ways in which the word "ideology" is used.[1] Only several examples will be indicated. We meet with ideology in philosophy and in the history of culture, in everyday talk, in political discussions, and in public opinion. On the one hand, ideology is used as a synonym for world-view and faith, particularly a religious faith (though this meaning of the word is not as common in German as it is in some other languages). Ideology is also taken to mean a description of particular programs, projects, plans, and goals. We speak at times of a European, or Western, ideology, or more commonly of class and party ideologies, which are frequently coordinated in a "main ideology." Ideologies such as these do not convey any sort of undesirable impression.

Most of the time, however, the term "ideology," and corresponding ideological thought, take on a negative tone. They are regarded as being merely theoretical, abstract, doctrinaire,

[1] Cf. K. Lehmann, "Die Kirche und die Herrschaft der Ideologien," in *Handbuch der Pastoraltheologie* II/2, edited by F. X. Arnold, K. Rahner, V. Schurr, and L. M. Weber (Freiburg–Basel–Vienna, 1966), pp. 109–180, with a comprehensive bibliography; H. R. Schlette, "The Problem of Ideology and Christian Belief," in *Concilium* (Glen Rock: 1 [1965], pp. 505–16; London: 6, 1, pp. 56–67). K. Rahner, "Ideologie und Christentum," in *Schriften zur Theologie* VI, pp. 59–76; H. Diwald, "Ideologisches Denken und Ideologien in der Geschichte," in *Klerusblatt* 47 (1967), pp. 73–80; D. Eickelschulte, "Ideologiebildung und Ideologiekritik," in *Grenzfragen des Glaubens*, edited by C. Hörgl and F. Rauh (Einsiedeln–Zürich–Cologne, 1967), pp. 245–273.

and, as a consequence, alien to reality. Ideology is played off against reality, facts, and experience, but it is especially set in contrast to science. This negative accentuation is sharpened when ideology and ideological thought are characterized as a prejudice motivated by specific intentions, leaving no room for an unbiased knowledge and judgment of reality, but rather viewing reality, partially or entirely, through colored glasses, imposing upon it extraneous motives, interests, viewpoints, and presuppositions, and then offering this perspective as the true picture of reality—as knowledge and interpretation. Furthermore, it is entirely possible that the proponents of an ideology may have no clear idea of the presuppositions of their thought, and thus do not examine them, but are convinced subjectively of their truth, accuracy, and value.

It is a fact, then, that the terms "ideology" and "ideological thought" are taken primarily to designate something negative, namely, the facts of an artificial or restricted view of reality—bias, prejudice; conscious or unreflective associations, origins, and forms of dependence; an outlook determined by a goal. We can recognize the distrust of ideology when, in intellectual disputes, the other side, the opponent, is suspected of being ideological, whereas the proper standpoint is understood to free from ideological restraints.

At this point, the term "ideological thought" once again becomes ambivalent. The question arises: does it signify a kind of thinking that projects ideologies in the sense discussed above, or is it a kind of thinking that discovers ideologies, brings them up for consideration, and therefore stands apart from them at a critical distance? That is to say, is ideological thought a synonym for ideological criticism?

These considerations suffice as a brief overview of what ideology and ideological thought can be taken to mean, and as an indication of the variety of meanings associated with ideology. We must now take up the question of the very nature of ideological thought.

II

Ideological thought, that is, the kind of thought which projects and articulates ideologies, must be understood from within the perspective of what an ideology is. On the basis of what has already been said, so much has been made clear, namely, that ideology is not, as the word suggests, a doctrine about ideas, but rather something that has a completely determinate conception of ideas. This view is a peculiarity of modern thought. It is significant, and by no means an accident, that the word "ideology" is a result of such thought.[2]

A comparison will make this clear. Ideas, according to Plato, the originator of the doctrine of ideas, are the fundamental form of being and the whole of reality, as presented and given in things. Everything that we come upon, empirically and temporally, in the world is dependent upon its fundamental intellectual form and, with regard to its concrete structure and actualization, is only a copy (and an imperfect one at that, because it is a copy of what is primary and real within the realm of change). The primary and the real exist in the perfect, timeless realm of ideas, the highest of which is the idea of the Good.

Ideology, as conceived in modern thought, presents an entirely different view: that ideas, and in particular their structure and creation in science, art, culture, ethics, law, and religion, are not self-constituting and valid in themselves, but are, rather, conditioned and dependent. This position is extended to hold that ideas and ideological thought have no end or meaning in themselves and are, to that extent, "free," but that they can and must be placed in the service of other ends.

That, in general, is the common understanding of ideology and ideological thought today. Ideology and ideological thought do not show us what is, but indicate what is to be sought, brought about, and attained. They are not "statements about," but "expressions of," or "means to."

[2] For the historical perspective, cf. K. Lehmann, *Die Kirche und die Herrschaft der Ideologien*, pp. 116–148.

This formal designation, *ideology as dependency*, as "expression of," still holds and carries weight in the modern understanding of ideology.

The various determinations of ideology presuppose that the realm in which the dependency of the ideology is grounded is itself differently determined. The dependency can come about in a number of ways. It might be an indication of the source or genesis of an idea; or a logical reference of the content of an idea to its foundation in certain external premisses or presuppositions; or, finally, an indication of the specific ends in whose manifold service ideological thought has been placed. No more needs to be said on this point.

The originator of the word "ideology" in its modern sense—the French Enlightenment thinker Destutt de Tracy, who took ideology to mean the science of discovering the intellectual faculties—sees the idea as an expression of the sense impressions that constitute it, on which it is dependent, to which it can be reduced, and through which it can be controlled. These principles were intended to lead to the education and formation of man and society.

Of not quite the same importance as the conception related to the genealogy of ideology is the conception, also formed during the Enlightenment, of ideology as the doctrine of the biases of mankind. This position is connected with the familiar notion of *idola*, the illusory images that hinder true knowledge, as proposed by Francis Bacon, and it is associated with biting critique of existing conditions in politics and religion. For Helvétius, the leading philosopher among the Encyclopedists, ideas are "the necessary consequences of the societies in which we live." According to his way of thinking (and he is following the lead of Machiavelli here, who, on the basis of such experiences, worked out a theory and technique of political action), ideas are nothing but a disguise for love of power. Religion and dogma thus appear as excellent means to be used by those in power as an instrument of domination, in order to justify and sanction the existing order and understanding of things as the expression of the divine will, or in order to prevent a change in the way things are, thereby blocking the progress of mankind. It is the object of enlightenment to see these connections and to unmask such deceptions.

It is only a short step from this conception to the most notorious and most effective definition of ideology, namely, as "false consciousness," as proposed by Ludwig Feuerbach, Karl Marx, and Friedrich Engels. They also propose the basic thesis that the concrete structures of ideas, particularly in morals and religion, are dependent on and serve what they consider to be the only determining reality, namely, economic, bureaucratic, and social relations in the process of production. Marx derives the famous formula that ideology is the "overstructure" atop the understructure determined by social factors. Ideologies are the mirror image and reflection of economic affairs, which are viewed as a "materialism." Religion is the mirror image of the capitalist and feudal order of society, and is possible only in such a role. They must serve as a justification of that order. This approach also holds true of Ludwig Feuerbach, for whom religion is the substitute (created by phantasy and the self-assertive will of man) for that which man is prevented from doing in real life. "The poor man has a rich God." Karl Marx explains, "Religion is the self-awareness of man who has not yet found himself, or has lost himself. It is the phantastic, utopian realization of human nature.... Religion is the groan of a creature in distress, the soul of a heartless world, as it is the mind of mindless circumstances. It is the opium of the people.... The critique of religion is the critique of the vale of tears, of which it is the saintly glow. The critique has pulled imaginary flowers from the chains, not so that man will drag his chains without phantasies and in despair, but so that he will throw his chains away and pluck living flowers."[3]

Religion, as the overstructure atop the capitalistic and feudalistic understructure, is at the same time an explicit protest

[3] K. Marx, *Frühe Schriften* I, edited by J. J. Lieber and P. Furth (Darmstadt, 1962), p. 488. For an interpretation, cf. H. Gollwitzer, *Die marxistiche Religionskritik und der christliche Glaube* (Munich–Hamburg, 1965). On Feuerbach, cf. W. Schilling, *Feuerbach und die Religion* (Munich, 1957).

against it; but it is a powerless protest, because religion accepts this position as an unchanging, God-willed given, allows it to persist, and flees into the solace of the hereafter, to the compensating righteousness of heaven. The struggle against religion occurs, according to Marx, because it suffers under existing conditions, but does not change them and thus leaves man, and above all the worker, burdened in his enslavement, in his self-alienation, with a system of exploitation. Moreover, religion prevents man from taking up the task of a necessary revolution (the reason why its crippling effect is likened to opium). The struggle against religion is the "struggle against the sort of world pervaded with the aroma of religion."

On the other hand, according to Marx, atheism and communism are not ideologies in the sense of "false consciousness," or flight. They are not a "loss of the objective world produced by man, but rather the first true becoming, the real actualization of man's essence—man's essence, as real, becoming real for man." They are, as Marx holds, "true consciousness." In classless society there will no longer be an understructure for religion, and thus this ideology will cease of its own accord. But Marx held that, for the sake of mankind, this process should be accelerated.

We have no intentions now of taking up a study of Marxism, or of pursuing its further development in communism (in which it is sometimes said today that Marx's famous statement about religion as the opium of the people was not intended as a definition of religion, but as a description of an historical experience[4]). Marxism, rather, will be employed as an enormously resourceful model of ideological thought in order to clarify the fundamental structure of ideology, namely, the dependence of the content of thought on factors outside of thought as given in the determination of origins and goals—factors which, because they are eminently effective, are called "real factors."

[4] For documentation, cf. *Gespräche der Paulusgesellschaft: Christentum und Marxismus heute*, edited by E. Kellner (Vienna–Frankfurt–Zürich, 1966); *Schriften zum Weltgespräch: Marxistisches und christliches Weltverständnis* (Vienna–Freiburg, 1966).

The fundamental structure of ideological thought was expanded in the course of history as new domains were discovered, whereby the dependence of the content of thought was exemplified, or, more exactly, in which it was shown how the production of thought lost its unique significance and sovereignty and became the expression of another reality which made thought serviceable, placed it in its service, and established it as means to an end.

Ideology is a dominant theme of the writings of Friedrich Nietzsche. In several of his writings, and particularly in *The Genealogy of Morals*, he disclosed the social and psychological origins of many moral values. "The slave rebellion in morals begins with the fact that resentment is itself creative and gives birth to values—a resentment on the part of beings who are denied the proper response of action and must comport themselves harmlessly with only an imaginary revenge."[5]

The love demanded and made possible by Christian faith is characterized by Nietzsche as the "subtlest flower of resentment," which grows from the stem of the tree of revenge and hatred, "the hatred that creates values."

From this point of view, weakness becomes goodness, fearful baseness becomes humility, cowardice becomes forbearance, and impotence for revenge becomes forgiveness. Conscience is not the "voice of God," but the "instinct of cruelty." Nietzsche assesses truth and the range of values according to whether they have a positive effect on life, whether they accelerate the "will to power." This latter value, and not true-false or good-bad, is the real criterion.

Ideology is also taken up by contemporary psychology and psychoanalysis. Sigmund Freud and C. G. Jung were the pioneers in this endeavor.

Here also the fundamental structure of ideology is retained. In this case it is the dependence of belief, of theories, of schemes

[5] *The Genealogy of Morals*, First Essay, Sections 8–10. Max Scheler's response to this interpretation in "Das Ressentiment im Aufbau der Moralen" (in *Vom Umsturz der Werte* I [Leipzig. 1917], pp. 45–236) has lost none of its validity.

of value, on intra-psychical processes and needs, and the tendency to accept what is believed not for its own sake, and for its truth, but for its significance, and eventually for its assistance with regard to the life of the psyche. An example of this is the acceptance of Christian and Catholic dogmas (such as dogma concerning Mary) by C. G. Jung not because these dogmas are true, but because he sees a correlation between them and the archetypes of the soul—especially the collective unconscious. Such circumstances constitute their "reality."

The negative results of ideology show themselves clearly in the fact that the spiritual reality of man may thereby be obscured, a situation that can lead to all the stresses, repressions, inhibitions, and illnesses that are the object of psychoanalysis. Consequently, these ideologies must be revealed for the sake of truth and the unrepresented reality of man, and his health.[6]

As did Machiavelli, the Italian sociologist Pareto sees in faith an instrument for domination in political struggles. Therefore, he reduces the entire realm of mind to a fundamental rationalization of interest groups, claims for power, and the justification of particular points of view. Truth basically signifies a function of currently successful power. The peak of this form of (total) ideology is reached when it is used as an instrument for the domination and control of the masses, and when domination of the masses leads to the repression of particular groups. That Pareto became the influential "chief ideologist" of fascism and other totalitarianisms is not surprising.[7]

We cannot at present go into other distinctions, such as Karl Mannheim's between particular and total, neutral and value-laden ideologies, or Max Weber's introduction of ideology into the social sciences. What has been said so far gives a brief impression of the problems that attend the question of ideological thought. It does not suffice as an exact concept of ideology *as such*, but it does indicate some of the elements that belong to

[6] Cf. R. Egenter and P. Matussek, *Ideologie, Glauben und Gewissen* (Munich, 1965).

[7] Cf. K. Lehmann, *Die Kirche und die Herrschaft der Ideologien*, pp. 124–126.

this notion, which have persisted through the developments and nuances to be found in the history of ideology.

We have pointed out that "ideological thought" is an ambivalent expression. It refers to the act and the content of the thought that goes on within the horizon of ideology, to the extent that it both creates and projects ideologies; but it also signifies the kind of thought that gains critical distance from ideology by penetrating the ideological structure, "unmasking" it, and working for its overthrow.

On the basis of these premisses, it is not uncommon to hear today that we stand at the end of the ideological era and are in the process of de-ideologization. Contemporary science (particularly the exact and empirical sciences, including sociology), as value-free science, is indicated as the way to free ourselves from ideologies.

In connection with these remarks, we should attempt at least some kind of determination of the nature of ideological thought.

Karl Rahner speaks of ideology as a conception understood as an entire system. The totality of ideology can be characterized as that which deliberately and thoroughly closes itself from the "whole" of reality and absolutizes one of its subordinate parts. Such absolutization of a subordinate part of reality takes place with a view to practical action, especially political activity.[8]

Paul Tillich distinguishes three uses of the word "ideology." In its broad, uncritical usage, it indicates a "system of ideas" as such. In its Marxist sense, ideology is the "creation of self-made gods." "Ideologies, in the strict, critical sense of the word . . . , are ideas that are produced in the service of the will-power of a group for the justification of local inequities."[9] Reinhard Lauth sees in ideology "a pseudo-scientific interpretation of reality in the service of a practical, social goal, which it justifies after the fact."[10] Ideology can also be viewed as a violent overthrow of the diverse pockets of force in a complex society. Then it may be said to consist in the "determination of a single, specific

[8] Cf. *Schriften zur Theologie* VI, p. 59f.
[9] *Gesammelte Schriften* VI (Stuttgart, 1963), p. 105.
[10] In K. Lehmann, *Die Kirche und die Herrschaft der Ideologies*, p. 138.

reality as a reference point among the pluralistic worlds of experience." Finally, we should mention the definition given by Theodor Geiger: "Ideological statements are those that appear, with regard to their linguistic form and explicit meaning, as theoretical statements of fact, though containing a-theoretical constituents that do not belong to the objective reality of knowledge."[11] Value judgments that result from emotional attitudes are offered as universally binding theories under the mask of a determination of the facts.

In order to diminish the danger of misunderstanding and confusion, it becomes necessary to ask, as soon as the word "ideology" appears in use, how it is understood, and how it should be understood.

III

We now have elaborated the premisses necessary in order to say something about the possible *criteria* of ideological thought. These criteria are related to the meaning of ideological thought which, among the various approaches, proved itself to be a pervasive constant.

The first thing that must be said is that ideological thought points out a real phenomenon by indicating the manifold conditions and implications of human thought and action. This is evident in man's concreteness, in his mind-body condition, in his historicity, in his status as a social being, as a child of his times, as a being who would rather play another role, a being who can be, and is, overcome by doubt and self-doubt.

Another aspect of ideology, one that is not always taken notice of in historical analyses, or made explicit in self-reflection, has to do with the fact that what is unquestioned, and uncritically accepted, is put to question for the first time; and that answers follow which reveal what has been concealed and disclose hidden refuges and repressions. The result of this operation is often a clear, sober, and liberating insight and determination that puts an end to doubt.

[11] *Ibid.*, p. 139.

Following are some of the criteria of ideological thought.

(1) First, as we have already pointed out, the acts and contents of ideological thought are not to be viewed as independent, free, valid, sovereign, determining, and primary data, but as conditioned, dependent, derived productions which are determined, according to source, origin, and content, by factors that gain their order outside of thought.

(2) The second, and perhaps most important criterion, is a more exact definition of what has just been said. Ideological thought is not concerned with gaining a knowledge of what is—examining it, interpreting it, understanding and expressing it—out of a love for truth. Ideological thought is, rather, led by interests and viewpoints, and determined by goals, which engage thought and require its service. Thought does not have to validate itself before the "in itself" of truth, but before the "for the sake of" of what is desired. Consequently, it is impossible for thought, approached in this fashion, to give norms and orientations to action. Thought takes its measure from effects, and its justification from practical use. What is "right" in such thought is not determined by ideas, values, or norms of justification, but by the utility of its goal. That is right which is useful.

(3) That leads to another criterion. Ideological thought is characterized by the fact that it is used to validate and justify the facts and circumstances of political structures, social and political institutions, political measures, and cultural tradition, and to protect them from the winds of historical change by surrounding them with the solemnity of necessity and obligation. What is given is seen from this point of view not as something subject to possible, historical change, but as an irreversible necessity. Thought produces this necessity, and often enough it is claimed for religion and faith. The "for the sake of" of ideological thought is all the more evident when historical or political changes arise. That which becomes a completed fact is given the aura of being the only thing possible, or the choice of the will of God. (On the other hand, there is the ideology of permanent revolution.)

(4) In ideological thought, there is no room for the reality of

what is immediately human and personal. That can be seen in the fact that ideological man is possessed by his idea, maintaining a reserved distance from his human partner, often avoiding contact altogether. This aspect is connected with the fact that ideological thought orientated in this manner is not concerned with what is proximate and immediate, but casts its view afar. It is more interested in secondary, external matters—with function, act, manifestation, and representation—than with the person and his irreplaceable value and individuality.

(5) In the horizon of ideology, thought is not understood as a personal act, as the spontaneous activity of a unique, individual, intellectual power, but as the disciplined, cooperative act of reflection which emerges in the collective anonymity that spreads itself over the individual and determines him to offer his own thought to, and merge it with, the collective reflection. On the same grounds, possible ethical decisions are "removed" from the individual, personal conscience by pre-ordained circumstances. The individual behaves correctly when he orients himself to the directives, the will, the "conscience," of the collective, and identifies himself with them. The "I" is replaced by an "it," personal identity by anonymity.

(6) Ideology, which is characterized by the fact that it either covers over reality or takes cognizance of only a part of it, nevertheless requires (and this is a criterion) a total adherence. It ordains over the whole. This aspect can be seen in the fact that ideological thought can furnish an explanation for everything, showing that it can arrange history, the present, and the future into the coordinate scheme of its dialectical system, so that everything appears as planned, prepared for, and prescribed. Everything is consistent and complete.

(7) On the basis of the criterion of total adherence, it is no surprise that ideological thought is aggressive and intolerant. Dialogue, frank discussion, and open questions are alien and strange to it. They are answered with universal principles, catch words, and "kill phrases," which are employed not to express or find the truth, but to cover up disturbing arguments with universal verities. Ideology is not concerned with engendering in-

sight, or convincing someone on the weight of reasons, but with influencing, subjecting, and surprising others—with conquering one's opponent. The most extreme means for the attainment of this end is terror.[12] Ideology does not function in the horizon of truth and falsity, but before the false front of friend and enemy. Differences concerning matters of fact are transformed into the fanatical methods that exist in personal enmities.[13] The other, in such a case, becomes "divergent," an "objectivist." Helmut Thielicke describes the state of affairs this way. Conviction aims at the existing order; ideology to the functional order. Conviction allows the person to be himself; ideology de-personalizes. Conviction allows for the other, personal goal. Ideology makes it into a means and an object. The person who is convinced asks: what is truth? The person caught up in an ideology asks: how am I to be influenced and how can I extend my influence? Catch-words become a linguistic method of de-personalization. The catch-word is not an expression of truth, but the instrument of the will to power. It applies itself not to the heart and core of the other person, but to his nerves and emotions.[14]

(8) On these grounds, it is characteristic of ideological thought that it remains unself-critical. This is so because it is convinced of the completeness and correctness of its system. But at the same time, ideology criticizes, judges, and condemns other people as being ideologists, and other systems as ideologies. The very suspicion of ideology carries with it a negative judgment. Consequently, ideological thought is not at all ready to admit its own errors, mistakes, weaknesses, or denials. These are kept silent about and not made public.

Because of its intense, fanatical aggressiveness and intolerance, ideological thought always manages to produce an opponent. It is always looking for a scapegoat to "take all the blame." Ideological thought builds opposition into its system.

[12] Cf. H. Arendt, "Ideologie und Terror," in *Offener Horizont* (Munich, 1953), pp. 229–254.

[13] R. Egenter and P. Matussek, *Ideologie, Glauben und Gewissen*, pp. 190–195.

[14] H. Thielicke, *Theologische Ethik* II/2 (Tübingen, 1958), pp. 31–87, particularly pp. 63–66.

IV

If we bring ideological thought face to face with faith, and more particularly with Christian faith, we reach the following conclusions.

Christian faith yields a direct interpretation of ideology. In ideologies, and the thought that follows from them, man takes upon himself (as seen from the theological point of view) the role of the "orderer" of all things. For ideologies are validated not on the basis of indisputable truth, or the values which bind mankind (such as righteousness), or on the basis of conscience, responsibility, or God; but rather on the basis of goals, interests, pragmatic effects—in short, on success. In ideological thought, man misunderstands his creatureliness, his obligation, his finitude and limitations. Man makes himself into the sovereign Lord and autonomous creator of all values and norms, as in the words of Genesis: "You will be like God, knowing good and evil" (3: 5). We can easily understand the oft-heard saying, that ideologies are the modern form of idolatry,[15] for in them what is produced, made, or willed by man is presented as the absolute ground, goal, and measure of all things, and the norm of all action.

Faith, as the response of man to God, who reveals and communicates himself, who has spoken and acted, who has come personally into the world and into history in Jesus Christ, whose word and promise, whose deed and work, lives on in the presence of the Church, the community of believers—this faith has often been misused in an ideological manner in the course of history. Moreover, the ideological alienation of faith is a constant possibility. This alienation is always present when faith fails to strive after its own clear representation and irreplaceable realization, fails to live from its innermost motives, and enters into the service of particular interests, aims, and goals, which are then presented as the necessary consequences of faith, and are attributed a validity equal to that of faith itself. The persistent attempt for an interweaving and equalization of faith and ideology lies in the

[15] *Ibid.*, pp. 66–68.

fact that faith embodies and incorporates itself in the world and in history; in the fact that it must create a form and structure for itself, which is itself a sign of its vitality. Then faith finds itself constantly facing the question of whether a concrete, historical expression and institutional articulation of the faith are the only possible, ever valid form and indisputable enunciation; or whether the living faith longs to risk an exodus from what has become customary and to seek new historical modes of realization—for the sake of the truth and life of faith. Insight into this differentiation of faith and its protection against ideological falsification is, today, the task and duty of the believer, and of the believing community. They must undergo a constant, self-critical examination of whether they believe, unconditionally and undisguisedly, and live in the faith, or whether they place faith in the egoistical service of their interests in the will to power, success, and prestige. They must decide whether they live from the faith, or from other sources and motives, which they garnish and conceal with faith and religion.

Faith itself, however, is, fundamentally and essentially, not an ideology, but (when it is correctly understood and purely realized) the unegoistical, free, thankful, serving, and loving acceptance of God, his glory, his will, his promises, his words and deeds.

Christian faith is not an ideology, because it is not determined by ends, but by realities and reasons—because it recognizes the grounds for its own worthiness for belief; because it is founded in the freedom and responsibility of the person as life and decision; because it respects the conscience of man and appeals to man as a person, not a function. Faith is not an ideology, because it exists not through the suppression and collective standardization of mankind but by recognizing the irreplaceability of the individual.

Faith is not an ideology, because it does not make man into a means to some extrinsic end, that is, into the bearer of an idea, a part of a whole, a function in a collectivity, or an anonymous foundation for a more decent future. It is not an ideology, because it recognizes the end and goal in man himself, because it acknowledges itself as a theological anthropocentrism, grounded in the midst of the Christian faith, in the incarnation of God. Man, as an irreplaceable person, is more important to faith than all "isms" and theories.

Faith is not an ideology, because it refuses to accept any absolutes within the limits of the world, however they may have been produced, and however they may be glorified. It observes the stricture of the first commandment: "I am the Lord thy God. Thou shalt not have other gods besides me."

Faith is not an ideology, because it is primarily not a relation to facts and formulas, but, in all of its articulations in writings and dogma, a confrontation between persons.

Faith is not an ideology, because its fundamental declarations and basic strictures do not stand in the service of human power and domination, or in the service of success and interests. Success is not a category of faith. Faith follows the sign of love, which apprehends its way and its obligatory archetype in the externalization of God and Jesus Christ, and which is characterized by the statement, "He who is greatest among you shall be your servant" (Matthew 23: 11). The friend-enemy schema, characteristic of every ideology, is radically overthrown in the universal love of God imparted to mankind, and in the worthiness for love that every man derives from this love.

Faith is not an ideology, because it possesses the capacity for openness, recognition, and dialogue.

Faith questions and challenges itself. It does not claim to know each and every thing. Questions, ignorance, provisional knowledge, imperfection, and incompleteness are among its basic elements.

Faith is not an ideology, because it can be realized in every social, economic, and cultural circumstance and condition, and in every historical epoch. It is not an ideology, because upon the disappearance of particular social, cultural, or political structures (ones which perhaps it has itself influenced), it is not itself caught up in dissolution, but can find new realizations in new forms without being faithless to itself.

Faith is not an ideology, because it brings about not expropriation, or the concealment of reality, or a flight from reality, or the alienation of man, but the disclosure of the truth of things and of human reality in its deepest dimension, in line with the principle that determines the reality of man, namely, that the more a man is present to himself, the more he is present to God; the more he is present to God, the more he is present to himself. And, only he who knows God, knows man (Romano Guardini).

What has been said in this reflection upon faith as the opposite of ideology will have been entirely misunderstood if it is made into a presumptuous triumphalism on behalf of the believer. It was intended merely to express the duty and responsibility which stem from faith and which are offered to, imposed upon, and promised to the believer, and to the community of believers.

CHAPTER SEVEN

Faith and Pluralism

THE THEME of this chapter is to be handled within the framework of a familiar pattern, namely, observation, judgment, and action.

I

First, the phenomenon of pluralism must be *observed.* And immediately we come upon a difficulty present in the word itself and requiring clarification, namely, that pluralism is to be distinguished from plurality. Plurality signifies the incontestable and ever-present fact that in the entire domain of reality, as it confronts us, and particularly in human existence, we find not only the one and the unified, but the many—variety and the manifold. The singular and the plural are adjacent to each other. Plurality is simply an attempt to make us aware of the structure of this state of affairs, to describe things as they are. The relation of the many and the manifold to the one is not considered in any deeper sense. Pluralism, on the other hand, is characterized by the fact that it not only recognizes the manifold, but also seeks to determine the relation of the many and the manifold to the one.

It is a fact that words ending in "ism" have a tendency to isolate what is being considered by taking it as a totality in itself. "Isms" have the force of "nothing but . . ." Someone has accurately remarked that "isms" are the contemporary form of polytheism, because pluralisms specify that nothing but the plural, the many, the variegated, the manifold, is true reality. It is fruitless to seek for, and impossible to establish, a relation to a one that binds, or coordinates, the many—a form of unity. A critical view would characterize pluralism by the fact that it does not rest content with plurality. Pluralism disrupts the connections and relations which constrain it, and "brings the many and the manifold into a reciprocally hostile opposition. This disturbance of relations is what we call pluralism."[1]

This is certainly the possibility of observing and discussing pluralism. However, the meaning of pluralism, according to contemporary usage, does not unconditionally fall under the extreme of "nothing but . . . ," although it clearly manifests a tendency in that direction. For in the concept of pluralism, the state of affairs that is doubtless being expressed is that the plurality of the manifold is the dominant and decisive factor in every dimension of human existence. Reality is constituted by the associations of the many.

In an article entitled "Pluralism—is there really such a thing? Objections addressed by a concerned contemporary against a word currently in vogue,"[2] Erik von Kuehnelt-Leddihn expressed the opinion that the trend of our times is by no means pluralistic, but anti-pluralistic. The author notes as an example the trend towards unity, collectivity, and conformity, for example, in politics, where innumerable factors are at play to reduce the many to a common denominator and to create super-organizations "which are constituted by the same, practically identical things." Its characteristic trait, in many different connections and variations, is *pan*.

The result is a typification and standardization to be found (and apparently to be found of necessity) in contemporary industry, technology, and economics, a standardization which can be universally extended through mass production and mass communication. This state of affairs leads to the uniformity of taste, consumption, style, opinion, and civilization, and, in the area of education, to an unmistakable tendency towards simplifi-

[1] W. Stählin, in *Pluralismus, Toleranz, Christenheit* (Nurnberg, 1961), p. 146. On the problem of the historical sources and aspects of pluralism, cf. K. Bosl, *Pluralismus und pluralistische Gesellschaft* (Munich–Salzburg, 1967).

[2] *Rheinischer Merkur* 1966, No. 38 (September 16, 1966).

cation. On the basis of such observations, the author concludes "We must suffer under no illusions. The world is moving towards a state of anti-pluralistic conformity."

Such an assertion, which questions the claims of pluralism as the identifying sign of our times, can certainly not be accepted without objection. Nevertheless, we shall not take up this problem more deeply, except to say that fundamentally we face a conjunction and dialectic of multiplication and unification, and that the age of multiplication has at the same time brought about the standardization of individual men. Rather, we must give our attention to a phenomenon pointed to explicitly by the author, who states that there is no doubt of *one* realm where the characterization of pluralism holds, namely, the realm of world-views, of faith, of religious and ethical convictions. Here, according to Kuehnelt-Leddihn, the private and the subjective are established as the norm. Here is where we find modern pluralism. It is pluralism as approached in this manner—ideological, *reflective, pluralism*—that is the object of the following study.

Pluralism, it should be noted, is relevant to world-views in a number of ways. We find here a huge, broad scale. On the one hand, there is the indifferent world-view of pure, scientific plurality, which adopts the perspective that it is practically impossible to find a comprehensive synthesis that would provide an overview, a universal coordination or integration of all points of view, amidst the differentiation and specialization of the sciences, their methods, and their languages. But on the other hand, a pluralistic world-view can also be highly applicable as a pluralism of convictions, of ethical "outlooks," of attitudes and ideologies which in their own way tend to a radical "nothing but..." Karl Rahner has described this situation as follows: "The real problem of the pluralism of attitudes shows up when particular convictions put forth a fundamental claim to universal validity which cannot be denied without denying their very nature. For example, a Mozart Society and a Hindemith Society, or an Entomology Association and a Society for Aquarium Enthusiasts, embody different convictions, but none of them seeks to win over every possible interest. Christianity, on the other hand, or a Christian denomination, or the ideology of the 'Humanistic Union,' or a party militantly devoted to dialectical materialism, in order not to deny their very natures, find themselves charged with, and bound by, a claim to the truth, and a mission to bring the universal conviction, the fundamental world-view, to everyone. However, the doctrine that there simply cannot be such a world-view, that such a universal claim is a priori and without question false, would itself be such a universal conviction with very practical consequences."[3]

The problem posed here demands our attention.

The task of observation implies a brief, historical *review* and *comparison.* Contemporary pluralism is distinguished from the epoch and horizon of a unified and homogeneous world-view of faith, as in the *one* faith and one Church during the Middle Ages in Europe. The "Christianity" of that time was the *corpus Christianum* in which the Christian faith was the point of unity for the whole of reality and existence, from both the individual and social points of view: in which the Church was the Church of the people (membership in one implied, without question, membership in the other: in which king and pope formed two arms of the same *corpus Christianium* and were unified, despite the gulf between them, in its service.

For a long time, Catholics in particular tended to regard this state of affairs as the *non plus ultra* of Christian existence, of the power of faith, and praised the Middle Ages, so understood, as the ideal time of the Church, unfortunately consigned to the past and present only to our dreams.

However, if we take stock of the historical reality without preconceived notions, we are compelled to de-romanticize this image and connect it with the oft-neglected facts that have been uncovered in sociological research. "The homogeneity of earlier, regionally bounded societies was basically, to a considerable extent, regionally conditioned. The great mass of people was directly and almost entirely occupied with the maintenance of physical life, and therefore their general outlook on things was

[3] K. Rahner, "Uber den Dialog in der pluralistischen Gesellschaft," in *Schriften zur Theologie* VI, p. 47.

necessarily fixed by culture. Over against the mass of people stood a relatively small leadership class which, at least for a short time, dealing with a regionally limited society, and within elements that did not alter the given freedom of man, could institute a homogonization such that divergent tendencies could, for a determinate period of time, be prevented from being objectified in society to any great extent."[4]

Moreover, if we take into account that education was almost exclusively in the hands of clerics, and was limited to them, and that the feudal system reigned at that time—which, because of the system of dependency it entailed, made the unity of dependency an unquestioned fact, even in faith, and not by means of personal decision but through social position and duty, as determined by milieu, origins, and tradition—then the contour of the situation takes on a different form. Our outlook on the Middle Ages, therefore, cannot simply be determined by the admittedly marvelous theological *summae*, or the cathedrals, those impressive, artistic symbols of the faith, but also by the equally incontestable "real factors" that had a role in the totality of the universal unity of the faith at that time.[5] We must recognize and admit that the price paid for this unity was extremely high, and at any rate a price which every Christian and the Church can only wish had not been paid. This perspective is all the more conclusive when we consider that in the *imperium Christianum* the non-Christian, the Jew, and the Mohammedan were viewed and treated as a minority, despite the official, solemn pronouncement that acceptance of the Christian faith was a matter of free choice. The situation was much bleaker for the heretic. It was impossible to accord good will to him. The goodness of the truth of faith, and its protection, were much more important for the individual and the community of Church and state than the goodness of subjective freedom and decision.[6]

[4] K. Rahner, in *Handbuch der Pastoraltheologie* II/1 (Freiburg–Basel–Vienna, 1966), p. 213.

[5] Cf. A. Mirgeler, *Mutations of Western Christianity* (London and New York, 1964).

[6] Cf. H. Fries, "Kirche, Toleranz und Religionsfreiheit," in *Wir und die andern*, pp. 173–207.

We could neither desire nor construct a Middle Ages as it is outlined in sociology and in the history of cultures. Its contemporary form would be a universal, ideological totalitarianism with the forms, methods, means, and consequences that are the complete opposite of a free world—that is, a world characterized by the differences which persist within it, and the problems which it faces. As a consequence, "the presence of a pluralistic society is a persistent fact, today and in the future, because the grounds for a non-pluralistic society do not consist apriorily in the absolute, objective correctness of a system or a world-view, but in historically conditioned social causes which have been suppressed and could reappear just as they once were only if the unity of the history of the world, or the freedom present in a rational and technical society and the social possibility of making this freedom objective, were to disappear. If the Christian, on theological grounds, cannot expect the global victory of Christianity in the social dimension, within the concrete limits of history, then Christianity can only expect a pluralistic society in its future, and accept it as its context of existence, or it will set up the conditions for a non-Christian, totalitarian society."[7]

The famous decision referred to as the Augsberg declaration of religious harmony, *Cuius regio, eius religio*, actually gave the choice of religious and confessional decision only to the lord of the *regio*. The *regio* itself, that is, the people living in it, had to agree with and follow this decision. If they had no desire to do so, only one possibility remained to them, a possibility that at the same time was a right, namely, emigration. That the *ius emigrationis* is not necessarily a cynicism, as it was (correctly) regarded at that time, but that it can be an ultimate point of freedom, is something that we experience in our own day. The rule, *Cuius regio, eius religio*, provided for a world to be divided into confessional and religious regions that were clearly marked off from one another. This situation no longer holds today, due to the fact that there are many religions in one *regio*. And this situation is, and is becoming all the more, the *one* world which, as we saw earlier, is represented by industry, technology, a

[7] K. Rahner, in *Handbuch der Pastoraltheologie* II/1, p. 214.

universal opportunity for education, communications possibilities, and internationality in research and teaching, and which is determined by the unity of history as a history of the world and of humanity and by the fact of a common destiny as well as an unavoidable solidarity in good things as well as bad.

We said that the medieval unity of a Church, Christianity, and world was not only grounded in a common faith, but was also, to a great extent, conditioned sociologically and culturally. The phenomenon today of a pluralism of world-views is by no means simply the result of the fact that this medieval form, understood as a sociologically and structurally conditioned unity, has disappeared with the passage of feudal domination, with the awakening and strengthening of nationalisms, with the gradual elimination of the monopoly of the Church in cultural and educational spheres, with the discovery of new worlds, new cultures and religions, with the emergence of the bourgeoisie, and later the working class, and with the various social, industrial, and technological revolutions. The unity of Christianity disappeared mainly because of intellectual movements. The passage of the social structure of the Middle Ages did not have to result in the plurality of world-views that we find today. It could, and should, have led to the unity of faith, for a sociological explanation of the passage from the Middle Ages to modern times must leave room and possibility within the reality of the Christian faith for Christianity and the Church. The way is clearly opened in the decisive anthropological declarations of faith, and in the task of the Church to be the advocate of mankind. The maintenance of the feudal system was not a requirement of the faith, but an ideological misuse of faith, taking what had actually occurred in history as a divine and unchangeable order, as the necessary form of faith and the structure of its realization.

The pluralism of contemporary times is chiefly conditioned by the schism in the western Church and the plurality of churches that resulted. The struggle between these separate confessions hardly measures up to the plurality of churches that is admitted in the New Testament. This tendency was accentuated in a divided Christianity by the wider differentiation of the free churches from the state churches, as well as by the multiplicity of Christian groups and sects.

Out of this crisis in Christianity arose, in direct sequence and as a matter-of-fact consequence, the phenomenon of growing non-identification between Church, Christianity, and the world. This phenomenon is evident in the emergence of the Renaissance, but it shows up particularly in the conflict between the Church and modern science. Science and Church were fundamentally alien and bitterly opposed one against the other. The polemics of the confessions and the wars of faith called for the mediation and authority of a neutral, political court. Moreover, attention was directed to new continents, cultures, and religions which revealed new and often startling information. The modern mentality arose amidst the application to philosophy of Descartes' suggestion, *de omnibus dubitandum*; the maxim of the Enlightenment, *Sapere aude*, "Dare to use your own mind"; the discovery of historicity and subjectivity; the retreat of the Church from a number of areas which it had previously laid claim to; the questioning of tradition; and the awareness of the integrity of cultural domains. This frame of mind led to the proclamation of the universal rights of man, among which the primary are freedom of conscience and religion, whose issue is tolerance and whose best realization is democracy. But it must be said that all the impulses and movements which led to, and best represent, pluralism are, when considered historically in their own right, not required by faith or the Church, but have grown without them, and often in explicit opposition. Thus it happened that the proclamation of tolerance set limits over against the claims of a Church that was regarded as intolerant. Marxism and socialism supplied the answers required by the economic and social situation of the emergent industrial age, by denying bourgeois society and the Church. Marxist socialism, which later developed into communism, and which has since gone through many dialectical phases and fundamental variations, poses the most intensive and powerful world-view in contemporary pluralism because of the permanent union it draws between a comprehensive understanding of the world and its radical alteration—

both coordinated via a critique of religion and atheism. (The problem of a possible pluralism in communism must be passed over for now.)

In order to complete this picture of contemporary pluralism, we must yet take up the question of modern humanism, which consciously seeks to become an atheistic humanism, a new Enlightenment, and thrives in many forms on several continents as a particular or total critique of Christianity, the Church, and faith. Since it is concerned, wherever possible, with undermining the position of Christianity, it seeks to play up the incongruities between articles of faith and articles of science, and to develop a true, atheistic *ethos*. Tasks and functions that once were proper to religious faith are here taken over by the exact sciences.

All of these things, and much more, lead to a familiar image. The world in which we live is no longer determined by fundamental ideas and institutions (spiritual, ethical, or religious), by universal tradition, or by common milieu, but rather by a complex manifold, a plurality of world-views. The Christian faith and the Church are now no longer the "one and only," but one among others—one among many.

That, in broad outline, is the cultural situation in which we find the Christian faith and the Church today.

II

We come now to the second level—*judgment*. By judgment, we here mean theological judgment which stems from an understanding of faith. Such judgment, however, is no easy exercise, since that about which a judgment has to be made, the very plurality of world-views, is unusually varied and complex.

Yet one thing stands firm. Theological reflection on this phenomenon, as it has to be made *today*, is different from that which would have been made *yesterday*, even though the latter still lingers in the pulpit and in the theology. Thus pluralism (used here as a general name for a number of "isms," thus subjectivism, rationalism, liberalism, socialism, atheism) was tagged as a collection of *errores* and condemned by Gregory XVI in the encyclical *Mirari vos* (1832), and by Pius IX in the *Syllabus errorum* (1864). The concluding sentence from *Mirari vos*, which held that the Church would never reconcile itself with the advances of modern times, became the guidepost.[8] There is no doubt that such expressions of the Church's teaching authority in the last century, which were ratified by some of the declarations of the First Vatican Council concerning God, revelation, and faith, have profoundly determined the normative limits of judgment asserted both within and without the Church. This evaluation holds also with regard to the judgment of theologians, who have viewed their main task as apologetics—in the sense of the rejection of errors, the refutation of false teaching, and the promulgation of the faith of the Church. Exceptions to such an overwhelmingly negative estimation and outlook—theological efforts to seek a point of contact between faith and the present, between theology and the contemporary intellectual climate—were unsuccessful because they were viewed with suspicion as a possible "collaboration with the enemy" and quickly silenced.

If we wished to characterize the declarations of the teaching authority and the statements of theology in the nineteenth century, we would have to say (without falling into a familiar pattern by automatically passing negative judgment on the nineteenth century and the relations therein between the Church and its theologians) that their exclusively negative viewpoint towards and consequent judgment of pluralism were one-sided, since, in the strict sense of the word, they saw only *one* side—that congenial and open to the Church and faith. This is understandable. For the cultural movements of that era were in explicit opposition to the Church, and expressed the corresponding consequences in word and deed. The answer of the Church and theology was reaction, condemnation, and resistance against these tendencies through the assignment of *error.*

However valid and understandable such a negative response to the pluralism of the times might have been (and there are a number of historical facts and events which could be cited in

[8] Cf. R. Aubert, "Religious Liberty from *Mirari vos* to the *Syllabus*," in *Concilium* (Glen Rock: 1 [1965], pp. 584–91; London, 7, 1, pp. 49–57).

support of that attitude, for example the highly questionable attempt to move towards an assimilation with the spirit of the times on the part of the so-called liberal evangelical theology of the nineteenth century and cultural Protestantism), it can be regarded neither as the only, nor as the ultimate, nor as a complete theological judgment. The qualification, *error*, by no means says everything that is to be said about the plurality of world-views. No determinate and established movement or ideology can succeed and persist on error alone. That is possible only on the basis of the light and *logos*, the truth, and indisputable values which also pervade the "ism."

If I am not mistaken, we are today at the point of attaining and revealing this fundament of truth. This will mean that a completely different response and attitude will have to be worked out, one that we shall now initiate. However, to avoid the opposite extreme, it should be kept in mind that we are not denying the error in this "ism." We shall simply no longer give it our undivided attention.

What we have referred to as modern pluralism has constantly sought to articulate its concern for *man*—his individuality, his freedom, his originality, his uniqueness, his power to prescribe with regard to the world that he confronts, his claim, as Kant put it, that he is not a means to an end, but an end himself, the conquest over possible self-alienation. These basic intentions, which we can identify with the term "anthropocentrism," are, as a structure, as an idea, as the will to an end, not in any way anti-Christian or anti-Church, but something deeply involved in the motives, ideas, and intentions, of the Christian faith. This conclusion holds even if the modern actualization of this anthropocentrism not only did not make such a claim, but explicitly separated itself therefrom, that is, if it took the opposite of faith and the Church as the condition of possibility of such an actualization.

The Christian faith, in its doctrine of the creation of the world, has de-divinized, de-mystified, and de-mythologized the cosmos and set it free as a finite, contingent world entrusted to, and given over to, mankind. In doing so, it created what we today lightly refer to as the "worldly" world, and thereby established the cultural premisses and general conditions for modern science and technology. As a consequence, they are not, of their very nature, opposed to or in contradiction with the fundamental facts of faith as proclaimed by the Church, but are the fulfillment of the charge to make the earth dependent upon man, and to lead the world, a world of becoming and self-development, to its determination and true form as the world of man.

That is not to say that all the objectivations of natural science and technical thought reveal, or seek to reveal, such a fundamental Christian structure. Often they are presented precisely as anti-Christian. It also does not mean that the teachers and theologians of the Church have in this connection either recognized or affirmed the liberating authority that is provided by Christian belief in creation. Otherwise, there would have been no Galileo incident, and much of the conflict and alienation between Church and science would have been avoided.

The anthropocentrism of modern times is certainly directed not only against the cosmocentrism of antiquity, but also against the theocentrism of the Christian faith. This attack is assisted not only by the representatives of new thought in philosophy, art, and literature, but also by the critics of this anthropocentrism, who only confirm what is being claimed, namely emancipation from the truths and strictures of the Christian faith and Church. However, neither side has had deep enough insight into the situation to proclaim that there is no necessity for opposition or contradiction between theocentrism and anthropocentrism and that, rather, there is a theocentrically conditioned anthropocentrism.[9] According to the declarations of the theocentric-oriented Christian faith, man is a unique image and likeness of God, the crown and end of creation, for whom the world was created and ordained. Man is destined, as the free partner of God, for personal union with God. Man's life and destiny attain the level of eternal validity. The incarnation of God in Jesus Christ, who came "for the sake of man and his salvation," the universal brotherhood that it establishes, the holy deeds of

[9] J. B. Metz, *Christian Anthropocentricism.*

redemption—all these things cast light on the anthropocentrism that God has willed, one that cannot be attained by any sort of anthropology.

Every form of modern pluralism that focusses on man and makes him its subject; that views the world as the world of the art and technology of man; that addresses itself to the freedom, indispensability, and inviolability of the person, as well as to the values and rights of human conscience, as realized by way of tolerance and humanity, and institutionally in democracy—such a pluralism is the original and legitimate fruit of the tree of Christian faith and life. This awareness is current and more active outside of Europe, especially in America, where it was able to develop and flourish free from the weight of the historic, ideological conflicts in Europe. Thus it is not surprising that at the Second Vatican Council the American bishops and theologians, particularly John Courtney Murray, were the most persuasive advocates of the affirmation of religious freedom by the Church. For it was in the context of religious freedom that the Church in America had attained its freedom and developed its far-ranging influence.

We are thereby led to hold that the Church, in passing theological judgment on modern pluralism, must not be deaf and blind to cultural genealogy. The proper attitude with regard to this situation should not be tears for the "thankless sons" who have grown up and gone away, any more than vain pride based on resentment, but understanding, patience, waiting, hope, and love. Karl Rahner's thoughts are worth considering at this point: "At least as naturally as the Church comes to recognize itself as a subject having a conscience inspired, guaranteed, and directed by God over against the world, it has the right and the duty to discover the image of its own future in the patterns of the contemporary situation, because in such patterns and in its reaction to them it discovers the anticipated effects of its own spirit. If the Church were to subscribe to cheap non-conformism, it would not only fall into the danger of sectarian narrowness, it would renounce a time that is fundamentally and specifically evidence of Christianity and the Church."[10]

[10] *Handbuch der Pastoraltheologie* II/1, p. 237.

These considerations specify the tasks for theological reflection stemming from faith and attuned to contemporary needs. The Second Vatican Council made the fulfillment of that end possible, above all in its own living spirit, which sought not to condemn, but to assist; which was concerned not with distance, but with contact; and which expressed itself clearly in several important documents, particularly in the *Pastoral Constitution on the Church in the Modern World*, and in the declarations on religious freedom and non-Christian religions. In these accomplishments the one-sidedness of the syllabus and the First Vatican Council was set aside. However, such insight into and acknowledgment of the truth in pluralism, and the very awareness of its fundamentally Christian structure, must not make us blind to the errors and dangers present in pluralism, and to the task of the prophetic word, preaching, and "conversion." That would be to replace one kind of one-sidedness with another.

There is, for example, an error in the supposition that a norm is established by the fact of pluralism, namely, that of a non-obligating, free-floating relativism whose fundamental principle is that, in questions of faith or general world-views, one man is just as correct as another, with the exception of those "who believe that they have found a truth possessed of its own objective validity, irrespective of whether it is accepted by anyone else or not. Pluralism then ushers in a pack of spiritually spineless human beings who choose to exist in a night where all the cows are black. No one would any longer dare to pose the ultimate questions of life. That would be an unbearably tedious world in which people would finally begin to long for serious intellectual conversation. Fortunately, we do not live in such a world, but in a world in which a man who wishes to live responsibly must choose whether to do so or not."[11]

That means that it is possible to accept pluralism as the world-view of modern society without slipping into non-obligating religious or ethical relativism, without lacking or surrendering the "distinction of being Christian."

[11] W. Visser 't Hooft, "Pluralism—Versuchung oder Chance?," in *Ökumenische Rundschau* 1966, p. 232.

Another possible error found in modern pluralism could lead to the desire for a new syncretistic religion out of all the religions —a sort of world or "esperanto" religion. This sort of thing has been attempted before, but has not succeeded because it is a product of fabrication and artistic manipulation. It has not lived because it is not grounded in life. On the other hand, any attempt to abolish religion and faith in every form and to place man in a world without God, ultimately founders on the fact that such a project goes against the fundamental structure of human existence, that is, man's radical relatedness to the transcendent mystery we call God.

Our reference to "errors" has only to do with the idea that it is important and necessary for theological judgment to look at both sides. Here again we see that only the whole is true. Theological reflection is stronger and more effective when it diagnoses error against the horizon of the acknowledgment of truth, and discovers indications and elements of truth against the horizon of the condemnation of errors.

But there is more to be said about a theological assessment of pluralism, if we take seriously the truth of the Christian faith, namely, that God at various times and in diverse manners has revealed himself (see Hebrews 1: 1); that the world, and especially men, because they have been created through the *logos*, are a word of God which man can listen to cognitively, and to which he can give an answer (a possibility that was not abrogated with the sin and fall of man, even though it was broken), since the questions and answers posed in the perceptions, experiences, insights, and ideas of man are "the grain deposit of the divine word" (or so said the Church fathers, who accept this qualification of Greek philosophy and mythology, and why should we not do the same with regard to contemporary thought, particularly in consideration of its greater richness?). The plurality of human experience, and its diversity in the mirror of the finite, reflect the manifold wisdom of God. It discloses reality as true and newly acquired knowledge. Thus plurality is not only permitted, theologically speaking, as the spectrum of the disclosure of reality; it must also be integrated into the Christian faith, because it reveals the possibilities and challenges of faith, and specifies its sphere of responsibility. Faith must attend to the truths contained in the plurality of world-views, holding open the possibility that it will reveal the true *logos* present there.

Moreover, pluralism, from the theological point of view, is a sign of the finitude and limitedness of man, an index to the fact that Christian man is determined by the other, by the many, by the community, by thou and we. He requires many and diverse concerns today in order to convey the aspects of reality in communication, exchange, association, and dialogue—the very aspects that determine his life and faith. "Only in God is everything one. At the level of finite creation, pluralism and antagonism are unavoidable."[12]

We have already pointed out that pluralism does not disturb the difference between Church and world—their non-identity, the autonomy and independence of the many domains of the world. It does signify the dissolution of the unity of "Christianity." However, this does not add up only to a loss. This phenomenon articulates the *world* as the essence of that *for which* the Church exists. It also specifies the independence of the Church. We come to a realization of the very task that defines the Church, namely, to be there for others, to bear witness, to represent. The egoistical temptation to view the Church not as a ways and means, but as an end, can thereby be found out and put aside, along with the temptation to substitute the Church for the kingdom of God.

Pluralism thus manifests the true situation of the Church, namely, as a Church in the world, in need of a world different and separate from itself in order to gain an understanding of its own uniqueness. As a Church in diaspora, as a "small flock," finite and yet the lasting representation of that of which it speaks, it is a "sign of contradiction." The Church is everywhere, and so are those powers in society which contradict the faith. However, this means that "social pluralism must extend beyond its cultural forms to religious experience and world-views. There is a need

[12] K. Rahner, "Pluralismus," in *LThK*² 8 (1963), p. 566.

in the history of salvation that Christianity be contradicted until the end of time. Thus Christianity regards pluralism not merely as a deplorable fact, but rather as something to be anticipated from the point of view of its theology of history and dealt with openly. To the extent that the Church must ever strive to win as many new men to the message of Christ as possible, it is working for the overthrow of religious pluralism and can never put this aim aside. But at the same time, the Church must reckon with the persistence of such religious pluralism from the point of view of its own self-understanding, and thus it can be calm and judicious with regard to this struggle. It has no right to take on the characteristics of sectarian fanaticism bound by the premiss that the truth is possessed only if it carries the day immediately, whereby it follows that one has the right to pursue the victory of this truth with every conceivable means, even if this victory does not at all involve the free, personal assent of the other side, but consists only in a political and institutional victory, which is never the victory of faith."[13]

The fact that, from the point of view of contemporary pluralism, the Church and Christianity are considered one among many others, does not mean that the Church must now regard itself in the same manner from the very point of view of its own unique, universal claim and mission. There is in the Church a singular that can never be reduced to a plural, but remains unique, definitive, insurpassable, and exclusive. This singularity is ultimately grounded in the uniqueness of Christ, in the non-analogous incomparability of his person, his history, and his action—that is, in the uniqueness of the Christ event.

In distinction from a sect, the singularity present in the Church as instituted by Christ remains open, related to others, to the many, to the world, which in turn are related to this one uniqueness without thereby abandoning their own identities. This singularity is at the same time the most comprehensive, the most universal, and most "tolerant," because it possesses the dimension for a catholicity grounded in Christ and the capacity for

[13] K. Rahner, in *Handbuch der Pastoraltheologie* II/1, p. 245f.

integration without absorption.[14] Thus the Church follows the path of Jesus Christ, the Unique One, who is the One for the many, the One for all—in the sense of the biblical "in place of" and "on behalf of."

The fundamental difference between the claim of the Christian faith and Church and the universal claim of every sort of totalitarianism, as seen in terms of the original difference given in Jesus Christ himself, consists chiefly in the fact that the Christian gift to the world, and its "presence there for all," are not a sign of violent domination, but of acceptance, before the offer of truth and love, of God's invitation to the world—an invitation reiterated at every moment in history. This openness seeks not the worship of slaves (something that is not possible in today's world), but the love of free men.

For this reason, the Church, through the pluralism of modern times, has in a certain sense become free, because it has been released from all sorts of obligations that historically it had been under. In modern times, much that belongs to the world has been returned to the world. The Church's freedom from worldly interests has, in the best sense of the word, de-secularized it, thereby opening and revealing the world in a new, less distrustful manner. As a consequence, the Church is free to represent the one necessity, without arousing the suspicion that it seeks to be the "one and only."

III

WE NOW come to our third point, which has to do with the *action* that stems from faith—the activity called forth by the challenges posed by pluralism. The premisses for this task have, to a large extent, already been mentioned and discussed.

First of all, a word should be said about what should *not* be done.

The Christian faith and the community of believers, the Church, should neither lament pluralism, nor be annoyed by it,

[14] Cf. H. Fries, *Wir und die andern*, pp. 181–183.

nor tolerate it discontentedly (perhaps as something only hypothetical); rather, it should accept it as the *kairos*, as the hour in which it must act and the world in which it must live and prove itself. The Church should not simply condemn pluralism because of the errors that it so openly displays. History has shown the ineffectiveness and inappropriateness of such an attitude and response.

Pope John XXIII had considered it a requirement of faith not to listen to the professional pessimists and resentful critics who label the present as the worst of all times and contrast it with the radiant, beckoning past. Nor should the Church imitate the prophet Jonah, who was sorrowed over the fact that Ninevah was not destroyed through his judgment and condemnation. That is not to say that the prophetic voice of the Church should never become a call for conversion and renewal, or a spur to conscience.

The Church and Christians should not, therefore, respond to the challenge of pluralism with any kind of resistance or defensiveness. It should not try to patch every crack and construct the Church into a citadel. A Church living in the faith should venture out into the clear field and open sea, cast out into the storm and waves with the conviction that it will not sink and drown.

Neither should it be restorative and anachronistic, seeking to re-establish a glorious Christendom or, failing that, a state religion. That is not to say that there should be no organizations or institutions within the Church; but they should not take the form of "pressure groups" and should not function without regard for the others. For what is clear and evident for Christians is not always so for others. Things should not be forced upon them, but rather should be communicated to them in the form of request, opportunity, or promise. Otherwise there will be, not authentic conviction, but conflict and mistrust.

It is to be regarded as fundamental that the Church and the Christian should expect less from institutions and organizations and more from persons and individuals—less from centralizations and more from centers, less from bureaucracy and more from man.[15]

The Church can no longer separate itself from the world, but is charged with giving itself to the world in faith, hope, and love, in fulfillment of God's gift to the world, which reached its incomparable height in the externalization of the Son of God; with the involvement of the Church in mankind, in the need for universal solidarity, in the preparation for a world of righteousness and peace on earth—as expressed in the encyclical *Pacem in terris*, and later affirmed in Pope Paul's *Populorum progressio*. The content of faith, therefore, must be prepared to verify the authenticity of man's words and deeds and situation. That is the true meaning of an "existential" interpretation, which seeks not to reduce Christian faith to humanism, but to make the relation of faith to man explicit.

The Church today must always keep in mind that Christological statements need not always be made into ecclesiological statements. That holds also with regard to the magnificent statement in the Epistle to the Ephesians, that "God had purposed to re-establish all things in Christ" (1: 10). This is reserved for Christ alone. It is neither a privilege nor a claim for the Church. The Church is not Christ. It is the body of him who is its Lord and head. To ignore this fact would lead to a triumphalism which would be less fitting today than ever before. These considerations help to throw critical light on statements concerning the "Christianization" or "return" of the world. The task of the Church is more accurately described as *koinonia* and *diakonia*, as the caring and responsible acceptance of the world, as so clearly expressed in the pastoral constitution of the Second Vatican Council. Just as important is the Church's role as advocate for the salvation of the world—a point also confirmed by the Council. In order that all may be saved, the Church must not take all unto itself in a superficial manner, but rather, in fulfillment of its very nature and following the example of the One, care for the flock of the few so that through them God will save

[15] H. J. Schultz, *Konversion zur Welt* (Hamburg, 1964), p. 93.

many. Its service is not made by all men, but for all men (J. Ratzinger).[16]

Among all the opportunities given to the church through pluralism, it is most of all aware of the menace posed to itself and to mankind by totalitarianism.

In what has been said so far, our stress has been chiefly on what the Church should not do with regard to pluralism. We have also considered most of what is to be done in a positive way. We shall now summarize those points briefly.

The fundamental mode of action for the Church must be *dialogue*—the courage, through self-trust, to enter into discussion with the pluralist world. The Church need not fear the concurrence of values and norms, nor be apprehensive about dialogue that touches on the theme of all themes: man, his world, and his future. No one has anything more important and helpful to say about what concerns man, his world, and his future, than the Church. At the same time, however, it cannot say everything that is to be said about man. The "One Necessity" is not identical with "once for all." Thus the Church must be open to and absorb the comprehensive knowledge of man and world that contemporary science has gained, and integrate it into its task. For faith must be related to contemporary man as we find him. If it has little knowledge or feeling for contemporary man and the world that makes him what he is, it fumbles in the dark. The dialogue between the Church and contemporary pluralism cannot be compared to a conversation between a doctor and his patient, but it must be a mutual exchange, a reciprocal relation.[17] Karl Rahner has thus captured the meaning of the dialogue of the Church today: "Under the premiss that the other side in the conversation also falls under the operative and saving concern of God, and thus that it does not, with all regard for truth and salvation, simply represent and manifest utterly false opposition to the mission of the Church, it cannot be the case that, in such a situation, the Church is only the church which supplies and

[16] Cf. J. Ratzinger, "Stellvertretung," in *HthG* II, pp. 566–575.

[17] Cf. A. Auer, "Was heisst 'Dialog der Kirche mit der Welt?," in *Wahrheit und Verkündigung* II, pp. 1507–1531.

teaches the truth, such that the only concern would be that only 'students' grasped it. The dialogue must be, rather, open and not destined to end with victory for the Church; for then it can have true meaning for the Church and represent a gain. That, however, implies that the Church, in such dialogue, is itself a learning Church, a Church that plunges more deeply into its own truth through dialogue, a Church that is always prepared, even when it is painful, to think through the old truths again, to free them from conjugate premisses, to view them under new perspectives, and to translate them, wherever possible, into the conceptual and experiential world of the other side of the dialogue.

"Reflexive knowledge of the dialogical character of its message in a pluralistic world involves new moral requirements for the Church than had previously held sway, namely, the courage to question itself; the trust in faith that all changes will take place within the lasting truth of Christ; and the humility that always presupposes that we must ourselves do a better job of finding the real truth so long as the other side of the dialogue is unable to accept it as his own, since under any circumstances no man has the right to assign the inability of his opponent to understand him to his greater stupidity or malice. In the new situation of a pluralistic society the Church must, in this sense, be the Church of open dialogue."[18]

Amidst contemporary pluralism, since faith and the Church are no longer maintained by milieu, tradition, or institution, and since the Church is no longer, as in times past, the obvious and unquestioned Church of the people, but rather the community of believers, it is essential to arouse the faith in its radical and total dimension, not only as the acceptance of certain statements as true, but as the personal and total decision of man, as the comprehensive foundation of one's whole existence in God, in his mystery, his word, his love.

This faith, however, must lay itself open to the situation and problematic posed by pluralism, and must come to understand the problems and difficulties with regard to knowledge which are

[18] K. Rahner, in *Handbuch der Pastoraltheologie* II/1, p. 266f.

found in pluralism, in order to fulfill anew the rule of *credo, ut intelligam*. Consequently, theology must take up the large and difficult task of interpreting, as well as presenting, the authenticity of faith vis-à-vis numerous questions and counterpoints.

Theology, therefore, cannot simply delve into the arsenal of previous answers. It must ever open itself anew both with regard to its norm-giving source and to the problems confronting it now and in the future. This is the way in which it becomes a dialogical theology. Thus it cannot merely reflect, it must "think ahead," it must be prospective. This is the basis for the critical function of theology in and for the Church.[19]

Faith itself, however, and the Church as a community of believers, become true and authentic through *love*[20]—a situation that is both an opportunity and a task to be completed. If faith means to ground oneself totally in God in order to enter totally into his word and mystery, this attitude becomes most concrete in love for man. Where love of neighbor is realized in its own unfalsified structure; where man, in the reality of life, offers and releases himself selflessly for the sake of his neighbor; where man holds nothing back and is prepared, circumstances permitting, to offer himself for the other—then is faith in God, in the concreteness of life, authentic as the ground of such a love. "Authenticity is nothing but love." The "demonstration of God" today can be accomplished only as a "demonstration of man." And if the community of believers is thereby also the community of lovers, of servers, of selfless assistants, a "Church of the poor," then the Church will gain the presence, in the midst of pluralism, that is its due, and the power that is manifest in the power of love. Because faith and love, from this point of view, are universal, the presence of the Church can also become universal. Then will faith and love enter into what Karl Rahner has called the "guardianship of the great adventure," of the widest possible openness and confrontation as the maximum of Christian response demanded by, and suited to, our times.

[19] Cf. Chapter Four, "The Critical Function of the Science of Faith."

[20] Cf. H. Urs von Balthasar, *Love Alone* (London and New York, 1968).

Pluralism, as a phenomenon in the contemporary world, should also arouse, as a necessary requirement, a legitimate pluralism *in the Church itself* if the Church is to be a world Church. The articulation of pluralities presents the Church with a great need for self-rearticulation, since until now it was chiefly the realization of unity that was sought and desired. Now the area is cleared and the hour is come for pluralism in the Church as a true plurality of its many services, functions, charismata, gifts, members, languages, and initiatives, and for the expansion of principles through the imperative, and of obedience through true responsibility, through the institution of a plurality that transcends what is western or medieval—a plurality that is not the opposite, but the expression, of unity, the very image of true catholicity and ecumenism.[21] The Second Vatican Council has specified such a perspective, and it is up to the post-Council Church to bring it to concrete realization.

This series of reflections will be closed with an ecumenical thought by Visser 't Hooft. He states, "For a divided church, the pluralistic structure of society in the world is too strong." A Christianity, he continues, "that spends so much of its time on internal conflicts has no sense of the correct perspective, and is therefore incapable of playing its role in the situations at hand. On the other hand, the realities of the pluralistic world bring the churches closer together. The pluralistic world tosses us all back upon the first principles of our faith, and forces us to take a new look at the world around us. Thus pluralism can present an opportunity for a new and unified witness of the whole church of Jesus Christ in and for the world."[22]

[21] Cf. the still classic work by J. A. Möhler, *Die Einheit in der Kirche oder das Prinzip des Katholizismus*, edited by J. R. Geiselmann (Cologne–Olten, 1957). And more recently, H. Küng, *The Church*.

[22] W. Visser 't Hooft, "Pluralismus—Versuchung oder Chance?," p. 241.

CHAPTER EIGHT

The Challenge of Faith in a Secularized World

The Prospects and Responsibilities of Ecumenism

I

THERE ARE many paths to ecumenical encounter. The one most frequently used is so structured that people meet literally eye to eye, and therefore put aside the isolation and seclusion that tempt them to work, whenever possible, only towards the confirmation of their own position. Such encounter leads of itself to conversation. Conversation of this kind is therefore a path to ecumenical encounter when it neither excludes nor conceals differences, nor is preoccupied wholly with their reiteration, but when it holds forth the prospect of moving towards a possible mutuality amidst differences, and when it seeks to view the differences against the horizon of community. Such an approach is by no means an unauthorized step towards the attainment of better viewpoints, but the correct manner of coming to grips with the matter at hand and the questions it suggests. Without a doubt, much has happened in recent times that suggests that better words and answers, and perhaps even better solutions, will be found than was previously the case.

Yet there is another path to ecumenical encounter—one that is precisely not face to face because here the road is mutually shared: with the danger, of course, that the wayfarers forget that they are making their way towards a common goal. This danger can be circumvented if a common viewpoint is determined among the pilgrims concerning the nature of that goal and the tasks which must be assigned to each to make that goal a reality. Such a mutual situation can therefore be, perhaps a danger, but a challenge as well: to stay on the path and not lose sight of the goal, and not stop by the wayside out of exhaustion or indolence or self-satisfaction. Further, this kind of mutuality can produce an encounter (indicative of the experience of human life as such) that is often more intensive and more effective than the sort we are used to. Thus we sometimes hear today of an "indirect ecumenism." Such a term can be allowed if it is taken to signify the fact of meditation, but not if "indirect" is taken to mean "figurative."

There is a concrete, historical experience to show how infrequently this latter sort of encounter occurs, namely, the ecumenical power that was released through the course of discrimination and persecution inflicted upon Christian churches and confessions alike, a situation that has been referred to as "thrashed-togetherness"—not a pretty, but an accurate description.

Although we do not find oppression and persecution of the Christian faith and the community of believers in the western "free world," the state of contemporary culture constrains us to relinquish all complacency and self-satisfaction, and to maintain, deepen, and reinforce the experience of common suffering amidst the common challenge directed at the Christian faith today—as a prospect and responsibility. That reintroduces the theme of this chapter: the challenge to the Christian in a secularized world.

II

Before we consider how it is that the secularized world, as a challenge, involves both a prospect and a responsibility for ecumenism, we must say something about what is meant by a secularized world. The word, and what it signifies, is ambiguous. On the one hand there is *secularization*, that is, the process of becoming secular, and on the other hand there is *secularism.* This distinction, which Harvey Cox, following Friedrich Gogarten, proposes in his well-known work, *The Secular City,* is important and helpful.[1]

Secularization, as the product of the process of becoming secular, means nothing but the common and established fact and truth that the world is not God and is not divine, but a creature entirely distinct from him, entrusted to the use and management of mankind. A free and independent world is neither "inviolable" nor "possessed" nature, but the world of man, the place for his free discoveries, creations, and plans, a de-demonized, demythologized world. A secularized world is one where man allows things to run the course which he finds willingly or tolerably suited to them, yet a world that he produces and structures, for whose present and future he bears the responsibility that it will become the world of man. A secularized world will serve man and him alone and be managed as a world of human happiness; for man is not a slave, but a free son and heir (see Galatians 4: 1–7). In this world, man is not the means, but the aim and goal. He not only has a capacity to understand his world, but (and this is something he has learned from Karl Marx) to change it. In this world there are no divine or demonic taboos. The word "impossible" no longer exists. A world-shaping omnipotence has been transferred from God to man.

In the last fifty years, thanks to the secularization, there has been more human progress than in all the centuries that are praised as the great era of faith and religion (when man despised the world and fled to the one, true, and most transcendent Good).

In a secularized world, faith—religious faith, belief in God—has no place, not only because it is not needed, since because man is totally involved in the tasks and responsibilities of this world, but because faith, as it has been represented historically by Christianity and the churches, has stood in the way of the

[1] New York, 1965. Cf. also F. Gogarten, *Verhängnis und Hoffnung der Neuzeit* (Stuttgart, 1953), and *Der Mensch zwischen Gott und Welt* (Stuttgart,[2] 1956); D. Bonhoeffer, *Widerstand und Ergebung* (Munich,[7] 1956).

emergence and development of secularization, struggled with it as a sin, encumbered it with condemnations and excommunications, and did everything in order to hinder this path of human progress.

Secularization, as the product of the process of becoming secular, is the name for an autonomous and worldly world taken up and structured by man, one that seeks not the kingdom of God, but the kingdom of mankind, one that extols not "eternal glory," but rather the glory of mankind.

Secularism, as distinct from secularization, the historical state of affairs, is at the level of a comprehensive, total world-view. It allows for nothing but "a secularized world." It is posited absolutely. From the fact that God does not appear in the secularized world, and that he is neither needed nor recognized in the laboratories of the basic sciences, secularism concludes that "there is no god."

In "a secularized world," the meanings that attend secularization and secularism flow together. However, there is a tendency that the fundamentally open phenomenon of secularization becomes more and more an exclusive and total secularism.

Nevertheless, the secularized world, which stands over against the Christian believer, is one with which he must practically cooperate for the fulfillment of his existence (and that includes his faith).

In both secularization and secularism, faith is posed with the so-called "God question." The twentieth century was once called the "century of the Church" (by Otto Dibelius in a book of the same title, which appeared in 1927). Before him, Romano Guardini had spoken of the "awakening of the Church in souls." This designation appeared to have been confirmed by the Second Vatican Council, which could be called a "council of the Church concerning the Church." However, even this designation seems to have been shaken more recently by the "God question."

Is this change in the context of inquiry, from "century of the Church" to the "God question," a loss or a gain? The answer must be that the change of context is a fact of history and should not be responded to with feeling, but with insight. So much is clear. The question of God is more important, more central, more comprehensive than the question of the Church. The sharpened question indicates the magnitude and intensity of the contemporary mood. The question of God does not make the question of the Church (or more accurately, the question of Christ) any less essential, but it does prevent the possibility that the Church take itself too seriously, in the sense of "nothing but the Church"—a possibility which had already been declared false by the Second Vatican Council. Moreover, the question of God puts the question of the Church in proper perspective, whereby it gains its true understanding. The Church is then freed from dangers of isolation, introversion, and self-formation. It is confronted with its origin, its determination, and its goal. It recognizes that it does not stand at the level of goals, but in the order of ways and means; it recognizes that the God question presents the Church with new demands.

If the Christian faith, through the challenge of the secularized world, is particularly engaged with the affair of God, this *kairos* is an ecumenical prospect and duty of utmost significance. For this challenge faces *all* the churches and confessions. In light of this situation, it is no longer desirable to attend to peripheries and to play up differences between the confessions. It is, rather, required to make the Christian community a reality. The God question engages the churches at their very core and impels them towards cooperation in faith and thought, in co-responsibility, in deeds that will permit neither rivalry nor pettiness.

The God question draws the churches and confessions together. It makes possible and insists upon new ways of encounter, for new searchpaths out of the maze.

III

Christians are challenged by the secularized world because it has called attention to the God question—a question that strikes Christians at the heart of their faith and existence.

How should this challenge be answered?

First of all, it should be noted that that sort of attitude which, in the name of loyalty to faith, consists in shutting off the secularized world, gaining no or only poor knowledge of it, is inept to say the least. Indeed, it is no response at all, but the refusal to give one. The same is true of any attitude that regards secularization simply as the raw power of sin at work. From this point of view, secularization is the culmination of modern history, which began with a denial of the Church, advanced to a denial of Christian revelation, and finished with a denial of God. Thus, in the name of faith the secularized world can only be condemned and rejected as its contrary opposite. Prognoses of the future of this movement point unanimously to dissolution, destruction, disaster, catastrophe, and failure. This proves all the more true in light of the fact that contemporary technology has made it possible to bring about the very destruction of the world and thereby take "doomsday" into our own hands. The secularized world thus can only provoke the Christian faith to the prophetic word that does not fear to speak of sin, judgment, and punishment. If faith, and the community of believers, refuse or are incapable of doing so, then they bring judgment down upon themselves.

Whoever regards secularization only in anger can only wish (there is no other alternative) that pre-secularization conditions were once again at hand, where God was immanent in the world, and where man approached nature with awe and piety as the appearance of the holy, and where he sought and found refuge and security.

They who instill such ideas and pose demands of this sort today in the name of Christian faith consider too little how much of their own lives is in fact based on the fruits and products of secularization. The apparent futility of their condemnations of the secularized world is interpreted by these prophets of corruption as an exemplification of the inescapable scandal of the cross. If the community of believers, the Church, continues to lose ground, that situation is sanctified with the image of "the tiny flock." There is simply no way to argue against such a position.

On the other hand, there is a kind of misconceived *aggiornamento* which identifies itself completely with the secularized world, conjoining secularization and secularism, rejoicing in both without critical distance or reflection. Such an approach to faith is radically disposed to eliminate every trace of divine immanence from religion, to propagate a religionless Christianity, to speak atheistically of God, and to replace every content of faith with profane anthropology. The glory of the Christian faith, its recommendation and authenticity for the present, is seen to consist in the fact that it signifies nothing of its own in particular, that basically it says only what the rest of the world has to say as well.

How it is then possible to continue to speak of a Christian faith is not altogether clear. Moreover, such a confession of faith can only expect mistrust and alienation, or perhaps sympathetic laughter, from the secularized world, unless it should come so far as Hans Urs von Balthasar's imaginary commissar, who remarks in conversation with such a Christian, "You have liquidated yourselves and thus spared us the persecution."[2]

In distinction from these inadequate answers to the challenge posed by the secularized world, we are to seek a *legitimate answer* as the answer of Christian faith. Such an answer consists in realizing that the fundamental phenomena of secularization—an understanding of the world as being independent and having its own laws and functions; a world at the disposal and under the responsibility of man; a world projected, produced, structured, controlled, and prepared by man for the future; a world where man is not a subordinate and passive slave or underling, but a creator and a master—are the effects and fruits of Christian faith, and more precisely of Christian belief in creation. This is true even if the ecclesiastical representatives of this faith—in both confessions—failed, at the time when it first began to emerge, to recognize its early intimations, and forced secularization to become aggressively defensive. This led as a consequence to the popular but false notion that Christian faith as such rejects the independence and autonomy of the world and works to hinder the mastery of men over the world.

[2] *Cordula oder der Ernstfall*, p. 113.

There are several incontestable facts to support the thesis that secularization is a product of the Christian faith, for we do not wish to make it seem that our assertion represents some kind of last-minute triumphalism on the part of the Christian faith. Only in a faith that proclaims the creation of the world by a sovereign, free, and transcendent God, and thereby places God over against the world; a faith that establishes the world as a unique, autonomous, and finite entity; a faith that coordinates the world with man and posits man as a person with a mind, freedom, and responsibility for the end of creation; a faith that, moreover, takes the world to be an historical world in process, striving for a goal—only in such a faith (which in Jesus Christ testifies that he has conquered the "powers and dominions") do we find the conditions of possibility for secularization, for the worldliness of the world, and for the hominization of the world.[3]

This approach also provides for a check-test. It is impossible to speak of a creatively structurable world in a system of thought that recognizes no boundaries between God and world, that disallows a commingling of divine and human, that views the world as an emanation of divinity directed to the world, that reduces God to the world and puffs the world into God. Such ideas were current in the myths and cults of ancient religions. But Christian faith, which de-divinized, de-mythologized, and de-mystified the world, was responsible for Christians being regarded as "godless," a charge which, among others, was responsible for their persecution.

It is a well-known fact that the Hindu concept of the immanence of the divine in all forms of life and their consequent inviolability poses great difficulties for the advance and progress of technological civilization. The cult of the sacred cow is a clear example. There is no doubt that the future of India lies in the pursuit of secularization. According to many Christians and missionaries living in India, this prospect also argues on behalf of the future of the Christian faith in that country.

To shift contexts, in a world-view or faith in which the world

[3] Cf. the discussions of these topics in *The Evolving World and Theology*, edited by J. B. Metz (Glen Rock, 1966).

is viewed as being without value, as an apparition, as a locus of suffering (as in Buddhism), there can be no impetus for man to intervene actively and creatively in the world.

Secularization is a product of belief in creation and belief in Christ, the Lord over powers and dominions, in whose testimony all Christians are united. (There is also a connection here with Judaism and Islam.)

This contention gains in concreteness when we recall the great and liberating authorization given in the oft-quoted phrase from Genesis: "Subdue the earth" (1: 28). It is then possible to see technology as a fulfillment of this mandate, a continuation of the sixth and seventh days of creation.

But to the extent that secularization is affirmed theologically, *secularism* is to be challenged and rejected on theological grounds. Secularism is a debasement of secularization (Gogarten). As an "ism," it is to be understood as a "nothing but . . ." It not only thereby denies its own true source in belief in creation, but it deprives secularization, as the free-positing of the world through God the creator, of its own supporting and liberating ground. In this way, secularism becomes a "world" refusing to accept God (as expressed in the Gospel according to John). It becomes an ideology positing itself absolutely, wholly unself-critical, blind and deaf to dimensions and realities other than those that it finds in itself, making man a captive in his own manipulated world and thus depriving him of the very things that constitute the true meaning of secularization—subjectivity, spontaneity, freedom, and responsibility.

Secularism must be denied for the sake of true secularization because, in distinction from the methodical self-limitation that is possible in secularization, it denies creation, transcendence, and the sovereignty of God; and thus man and the ultimate realities that are to be found in the technological world.[4] A rejection of secularism for the sake of secularization seeks to preserve for man a realization of *humanum*, that human and personal dimension which cannot be manipulated. This realization cannot be

[4] H. Urs von Balthasar has done the most significant work in this area, primarily in *Die Gottesfrage des heutigen Menschen* (Vienna, 1956).

gained from science and technology as such. It is a question of responsibility, of an unconditional duty arising out of perfect means and confused ends—a duty that, needless to say, can be performed only if the unconditional is directly reflected upon and mediated. Here we have the fullness of the concrete ethical question: should we do what technology has made it possible for us to do? How do we gain control over our technological power? Where are the norms and limits of human freedom—the authority to do what should be done? And what should be done? What is the norm of righteousness and freedom, the ground of the inviolability of human dignity? Furthermore, is it permissible, by subscribing without critical distance to a superficial and naïve optimism in progress, to hold that satisfaction can be attained if only the functions of technology are perfected, but at the same time be blind to the limitations that are present in every human work? Can we be blind to the reality of evil in the sentiments, mind, and heart of man, whereby the noblest perfections become the means of disaster? Can we be blind to the reality of what the Christian faith calls sin? Can we refuse to heed the lesson of the cross of Christ?

The Christian faith is challenged to become the advocate for questions which no laboratory, no experiment, no computer can solve—questions which, nevertheless, hold the fate of the world in balance. Faith cannot allow itself to be intimidated in face of this task. For by posing such questions it fulfills its role as the conscience of the secularized world. That means that true secularization is possible only if these questions are taken up and given full attention—something that secularism refuses to accept. In light of this situation, the entirety of the Christian faith is always at the focus of inquiry. That is its prospect and responsibility in the contemporary world. The pastoral constitution of the Second Vatican Council has addressed itself to this situation in very moving terms.

Out of these reflections the function of the Christian faith becomes clear, namely, not to represent everything, but the One Necessity; not to be the world, but the salt of the earth, and the light of the world, the light on the paths of mankind. That is not a presumptuous claim, but an offer and a duty. And it cannot be taken up by just anyone—only by *one* who has heard the will of God distinctly in the *word of faith.* Faith and the community of believers, the Church, are not intent on dominion, but on humble service to the world. It is thus impossible for a Christian to renounce the prospect of a truly secularized and hominized world.

It is also possible that the anthropological aspects and disclosures of the Christian faith could bring about a convergence of the words and answers of the Christian faith among the Christian confessions, and thus act as an ecumenical force.

It thus becomes clear how intense, how central, how radical Christian witness is at this point, when confessional differences are to be put aside in favor of that Christian reality which all Christians acknowledge—belief in God, the creator of heaven and earth, in Jesus Christ, *Logos* and *Kyrios,* the Son of God and Brother of all men, and in the Holy Spirit, the Lord and Giver of life.

IV

We have noted that the uniqueness of the secularized world consists in the fact that it dissolves the undifferentiated unity of Church and world, and thus becomes obviously the opposite of both. We have also noted, with regard to this differentiation, that it is not to be deplored or condemned, nor is it to be peevishly tolerated, but accepted as a prospect and a responsibility of the Christian faith. If that is the case, then it comes about of necessity that the Christian faith must seek to initiate and enter into dialogue with the secularized world. Although the term "dialogue" is overworked today, this fact should not lead to a false impression that everything has already been done and completed in this regard.

The themes of this dialogue have already been indicated, and we have seen too that it is all the more urgent to pursue this dialogue at once, since there was no dialogue when there should have been: at the beginning, during the decisive phases of secularization, before there was alienation and mutual distrust on either side. Today, the task of dialogue is aimed precisely at overcoming such feelings of alienation and mistrust.

However, dialogue is not desirable only because faith has something valuable to say to the secularized world, but chiefly because faith and the community of believers must take upon themselves the realities disclosed in and by the secularized world. These largely concern man and the world of contemporary man. Faith must become related to them and must vindicate and authenticate itself in them if it is to be living and effective. A Church that seeks to serve mankind is in need of the service of mankind. A Church that does not listen to the world must answer to a world that does not listen to the Church.

The sciences of the secularized world have disclosed realities, made discoveries, and shattered ideologies, taboos, and superstitious ideas. In these accomplishments it has performed a service to truth and to mankind that cannot be overlooked by the Christian faith and the Church. In its pastoral constitution the Council said explicitly that "in its living relationship to the world, the Church must continue to mature with the experience of history" (art. 43). That is true above all because the true and deepest theme of modern science, including the natural sciences, is man. Christian faith cannot carry out its service to mankind if it does not know man, or has made a false image of him. The statements of the Christian faith are related to concrete and historical man. Today that means man in the secularized world.

Consequently, the dialogue of the Church with the world is a two-sided conversation, where both sides not only speak and teach, but listen and learn; where a living exchange takes place, each side contributing what it has.

The dialogue between the community of believers in the faith and the secularized world should not merely have to do with theory, interpretation, and information, but should expand to the level of *cooperation*. This is especially the case since the secularized world today is interested in the human world, organizing itself against poverty, disease, hunger, injustice, racial prejudice, dissension, war, and ignorance. When the secularized world is so moved out of humanity and brotherhood, the Church cannot stand off to the side, ill-tempered or content to play the role of arbiter and judge.

The Church, as the community of believers, must attain solidarity with such an involved world and cooperate with all of its efforts. It should not be disturbed over the fact that much more is being accomplished now than in earlier times, when Christianity and the Church were the dominant powers. Rather, it must rejoice over the fact that the primary tasks of believers are being accomplished with regard to the realization of happiness, justice, love, and mercy. The Bible takes note of the surprised and sullen reaction of the disciples when an "alien exorcist" cast out the powers of evil. They wanted to forbid him, "because he does not follow with us." Jesus answered, "Do not forbid him; for he who is not against you is for you" (Luke 9: 49f.). These words should be kept in mind when, in the name of Marxism and communism, the powers of evil, in the form of social injustices, are cast out. The community of believers in the faith must not wish that less humanitarianism and brotherhood, less social concern and aid, will take place in the name of Marxism and communism, so that the true state of affairs will show up starkly against a dark background and upon a mass of ruins. On the contrary, faith should rejoice over every advance towards the realization of humanity and thereby take notice of a real challenge in the true unity of the love of God and the love of neighbor, as expressed in the First Epistle of St. John: "How can he who does not love his brother, whom he sees, love God, whom he does not see?" (4: 20). The words of Jesus, "As long as you did it for one of these, the least of my brethren, you did it for me," and "As long as you did not do it for one of these least ones, you did not do it for me" (Matthew 25: 40. 45), still hold true.

If the Christian faith grows authentically primarily through selfless love,[5] and if its prospect and responsibility lie here, then it can also be said that wherever selfless and brotherly love are

[5] Cf. H. Urs von Balthasar, *Love Alone*.

practiced, wherever the peacemakers are at work, wherever dehumanization is overthrown, that is where the identifying mark of Christ is visible, where there is a union with the faith that bears witness to Jesus Christ, the faith that is peace (see Ephesians 2: 14) and is identified with the lowest brothers of man.

This perspective adds understanding to what is spoken of today as "anonymous Christianity." However, it is perhaps doubtful to say that non-Christians have for such a long time absorbed so much Christianity into themselves that our world is "a world filled with Christ far beyond the pale of official Christianity,"[6] and with good grounds.

The community of believers in the Christian faith should carry out such cooperation, ever more intensively than before, because the secularized world affirms and accepts this cooperation. There are clear signs in support of this contention, even within the evolution of Marxism and communism, which are concerned more and more with moving away from a complete restriction of anything that has to do with faith, religion, and the Church and towards dialogue,[7] and are convinced that the human world cannot be built without, or in opposition to, the Christian faith. The words of John XXIII, in *Pacem in terris*, and Paul VI, in *Populorum progressio*, have met with world-wide acceptance, in many cases an acceptance greater than that given in the Church itself. The same can be said concerning the efforts of the Church for peace. That they met with no greater success is no argument against them.

Insofar as the world realizes what is the deepest duty of the Christian faith itself, this faith is not superfluous. On the contrary, it must persist, and then be called into account. For only in this faith is the ultimate ground of a universal and unlimited love opened up, a love that includes love of enemies and finds its

[6] Cf. J. C. Hampe, *Die Autorität der Freiheit* III, p. 175.

[7] Cf. particularly R. Garaudy, "Vom Bannfluch zum Dialog," in Garaudy, Metz, and Rahner, *Der Dialog oder Ändert sich das Verhältnis zwischen Katholizismus und Marxismus?* (Reinbeck-Hamburg, 1966), pp. 27–118.

greatest triumph in reconciliation. The statements of the Christian faith are the inexhaustible source of kindness among men that otherwise would not exist.

The Church must also cooperate with the secularized world in a concern for the formation of the future. The ultimate future in which the Christian faith hopes has to do with the second coming of Christ in glory, the kingdom of God, the state where "God is all in all" (1 Corinthians 15: 28). This absolute future is not identical with a world produced by man, but rather is the creative work of God. The "new Jerusalem," as Harvey Cox states explicitly, is not the prolongation of the "secular city." However, this ultimate future is joined to the mandate and duty to make the world into a human world, the inhabited earth into a habitable earth, and to do everything possible to reform attitudes and alter conditions in order that de-humanization may be avoided and the world become a world of peace and brotherhood.

We should also take note of the fact that it is part of the mission of the Christian faith to inspire mankind with a sense or consciousness of being part of a family. More precisely, this mission can be advanced through fostering the realization that all men are children of God. In the Council's *Dogmatic Constitution on the Church*, the Church is understood primarily as a *mysterium*. That consists primarily in the fact that the Church is a sacrament, that is, a visible and operative sign of the unity between God and man, and of the unity among men which it makes possible.

The maintenance of a precise distinction between Christian hope and hope for human progress through science and technology will work to remedy utopian or disillusioned thought about progress in the world and those things which progress cannot always or necessarily or ever defeat: suffering, tragedy, failure, and death. These are the things which form the perpetual ground for the dread and doubt that pervades the secularized world; these are realities that can be overcome only by the power of Christian hope. For this hope is based on the conquest of death. It has its origin in the resurrection of Christ from the dead, from which it derives its limitless power.

From these remarks, it is sufficiently clear how deeply related are the secularized world and the Christian community, how much support and assistance they can give to each other in the service that is their common duty—service to the world and to mankind, which are not the opposite, but the object, the recipient of Christian faith.

The challenge to Christians in the secularized world, in its ecumenical prospect and responsibility, must be responded to in such a way that the Church (which must never become isomorphic with the world) must proceed into the actual world in order to be able to be the Church in and for this world—in and for the ever concrete and historically conditioned world, today's secularized world. The Church (which bears historicity as one of its own essential traits) has always entered into the conditions and structures of the historical situation. This circumstance has had a profound effect on its image and structure. Further, such a procedure is quite legitimate, and is portentous only when no exodus is attempted when the historical situation is checked and grows rigid even though the hands of the clock have long since moved on.

Applying these considerations to the present, it is the case that the Church, if it wishes to be contemporary, must be determined by traits that are deeply its own even though they are not always represented historically. They are: *diakonia*, *martyria*, *koinonia*, preparedness for service, humanity, brotherhood, and hospitality.

In the Church itself, therefore, in the community of believers, there must be first of all room for freedom, spontaneity, initiative, and responsibility. Love that is realized in the Church must be exemplary and contagious.

Thus the Church in the secularized world must be careful to avoid any kind of self-centered salvationism, from any striving for power, prestige, and privilege, from any condescending attitude of triumph, from doctrinaire or overbearing postures. The Church today must part with any inappropriate (and pathetic) desire to know everything better than everyone else; it must show as well any belief in the almighty power of organization and institution. The Church must be involved as the people of God. Its symbol is not the ark of Noah, the house of glory, the cathedral. These figurations once had their high, impressive legitimate historical meaning, but not as the product of eternity, but of time. The symbol of the Church today is the canopy of God beneath man. And the cross must symbolize the being and action of the Church with new force—as the sign of the vertical dimension uniting God and man, and the horizontal dimension extending into the world and directed in love to all mankind. From all of this there emerges a new and more comprehensive image of the Church, one that is not greater in magnitude, but richer in inner fullness and dimension.

The more completely these realities are present in the community of believers, the more will the word of faith of the Church be listened to as prophetic, directive, and supporting—as the conscience of the world, as the demand of God, as light, as responsibility, as concern and promise, as the Word of the cross—the word that is prophecy, that remains a folly and a scandal, that cannot be put aside in any dialogue.

The more that Christians follow these paths towards a "conversion of the world,"[8] as the after-effect of God's gift to the world that was fulfilled in God's entrance into the world as man, as Christ, and remains present in the world through the Church, the more will it succeed in leading the secularized world away from radical secularism, and bring about the *conversion of the world to God.* This is the only possible answer to the fact that God has given himself to the world in creation, in love, and in his Son.

The more that Christians of all confessions take up the challenge posed by the secularized world, and the great prospect and responsibility that it entails; the more they understand that this task hinges not on the points of difference between the various confessions, but on their community and centrality in faith; the more they pay heed to their common goal, the more will the confessions move forward together as a whole in real, courageous encounter—in faith and trust, in hope and love.

[8] H. J. Schultz, *Konversion zur Welt* (Hamburg, 1964).

CHAPTER NINE

Faith and Atheism

I

DESPITE OBVIOUS difficulties it seems fitting to begin our theological reflection on atheism with reference to statements from the Second Vatican Council—even though there are signs that a reactionary trend is taking form in the Church in the name of that Council. Our procedure is not meant to imply that theology should now concern itself chiefly or only with being a faithful exemplification of the conciliar documents. We ground ourselves there simply because the phenomenon of modern atheism has been given clear expression and focus within the conciliar texts. Of course, the theological orientation that we shall seek to develop must also take into account those various theological perspectives which are associated with a return to biblical sources, with insights into history and the contemporary cultural situation, with modern anthropology, psychology, sociology, language, and so forth.

We have already indicated that black-and-white distinctions cannot be used as a hermeneutical rule for Council statements. What is new is not to be glorified for the sake of its newness, nor what is old to be treated with contempt because it is old. The Council was concerned with uniting continuity with advance, tradition with the new, out of a deep appreciation of true historicity and the contemporary situation with regard to faith.

Atheism must be taken up in conjunction with themes that have to do with the distinction between past and present. What is new does not consist in the revocation or rejection of what has previously been the case, but in the development of new or hitherto neglected features. This state of affairs will be considered in what follows.

Atheism has always been regarded as an "ism," that is, as a doctrine, a teaching, a theory, a philosophy, or a world-view. In support of this observation we need only examine the cursory, almost simplified treatment given to atheism in Denzinger, or in the encyclicals of the popes, or in nearly any theological encyclopedia or textbook in apologetics or dogmatics. Atheism was described by the First Vatican Council as the denial of a true God, the Creator and Lord of all visible and invisible things (Denzinger, 3021). This position was intensified by the anathema that was put upon those who, as it is stated, are not ashamed to assert that there is nothing but matter (Denzinger, 3022).

Atheism was also taken up against the horizon of the knowledge of God. Thus "God, the ground and goal of all things, can be known with certainty from a consideration of created things through the natural light of human reason" (Denzinger, 3004, 3026). Behind this particular stress lay perhaps the notion that once the possibility of knowledge of God is solved, the phenomenon of atheism will disappear of itself. This appeared quite an easy proof to accomplish since, in classical theology and philosophy, especially in scholasticism, many ways were offered whereby one could negotiate the leap from world to God. Thus atheism was chiefly qualified as a theory, though having certain practical consequences, which had to be approached theoretically, or, more precisely, philosophically. Atheism was classed as the culmination of the "pernicious errors of the time." It was described as the source of the many disastrous effects in all forms of thought, life, and action. Further, it was declared that atheism is always culpable, that it cannot be accepted by individuals without guilt. This guilt was specified as the *hybris* of mankind, manifested in modern times above all by autonomy and the subjectivism that it entails. The textbooks made a distinction between theoretical and practical, or positive and negative, atheism, but again this was only a doctrinal or theoretical differentiation. Further this position was linked with the conviction that the atheist "cannot maintain a sincere, doubt-free persuasion in the non-being of God for long, for the idea of God forces itself upon us too strongly in the consideration of nature and other matters and meets a too deeply rooted need of the soul."[1]

This view of atheism, as presented by educators and theologians *before* the Second Vatican Council, regarded it primarily as a theory and doctrine in sharpest contradiction to Catholic doctrine, one confronted in various forms of negation, struggle, and radical denial. Thus any response to atheism was always necessarily theoretical.

The Church and theology were in no position critically to assess and challenge themselves through atheism so completely their contrary. Both proffered their directives, and worked out their points of view, on the basis of a position that was completely certain. Their approach was one of negation, judgment, resistance, and struggle, carrying with it the absolute guarantee of final victory. Educators and theologians declined even to take up eventual questions and matters of provocation, for that might have been understood as treason, compromise, or uncertainty—and that, of course, meant that it was entirely possible that answers had been given to questions that were never asked, or that positions had been drawn up for which there may have been nothing corresponding in actuality to what had been characterized. Thus, not unusually, the Church was again doing battle against a caricature, against atheistic positions that had never been held.

II

A characteristic of some of the important statements on atheism of the Second Vatican Council was that they viewed the phenomenon of atheism as having ramifications and aspects other than those which had previously been recognized and considered by theology and the Church.

(1) First of all, it is important to note that the theme of

[1] F. Kiekamp, *Katholische Dogmatik nach den Grundsätzen des heiligen Thomas* I (Munster, 1934), p. 109.

atheism, although of much greater theological depth than hitherto recognized, is to be found not in a dogmatic constitution, but in the *Pastoral Constitution on the Church in the Modern World.*

This is a clear indication that the phenomenon of atheism is viewed not simply as theory or doctrine, but also as a concrete existential phenomenon in the contemporary world. In other words, atheism is not merely regarded as one "ism" among others, but is confronted primarily in the form of concrete men who are atheists. It follows, then, that the Church is not primarily concerned with theological, disciplinarian, or spiritual strategy against an alien power, marching forth in the armor of infallibility, but that it is open to and listens to the questions of the contemporary world, even if these questions are uncomfortable, agonizing, shameful, or painful.

Finally, the inclusion of atheism in a pastoral constitution, that is, in a statement concerning the tasks of pastoral duty, means that it is not enough to declare that "the Church is opposed," that atheism and Christian doctrine are poles apart; to marshall out the familiar images of fire and water, light and darkness, and believe that something is thereby accomplished. Rather, it is required to take up the matter, or better, to receive the men and the human communities who profess the matter, and to be challenged and questioned critically through the phenomenon of atheism as it has arisen in the midst of Christianity. One must be ready to pass judgment, not on others, but on oneself; to pose the question of guilt, not to others, but to oneself. The correlation between the phenomenon of atheism and pastoral matters should not be taken as a sentimental melodrama, as a dispensation or flight from theology. Properly understood, the care of souls is a sort of applied theology, its critical test.

(2) The Council has undertaken a *diagnosis* of atheism, viewing it neither, as was the case previously, as an exception to the rule, as *insania paucorum* (Augustine), as the pure incarnation of evil and the satanical that plunges believers into fear and trembling, or as the offspring of folly; nor merely as a false viewpoint in the realm of knowledge and cognition. Rather, atheism is viewed as a mode of existence which is not so much a theme

as a premiss for atheists, and which thus is a deeply grounded and universal phenomenon. Walter Dirks has made the penetrating observation that the fact that there are so few declared atheists attests to the power of contemporary godlessness. The same can be said of the post-atheistic phase that we have already entered.

There is a relevant Council statement in this regard: "... the denial of God or of religion, or the abandonment of them, are no longer unusual and individual occurrences. For today it is not rare for such decisions to be presented as requirements of scientific progress or of a certain new humanism. In numerous places these views are voiced not only in the teachings of philosophers, but on every side they influence literature, the arts, the interpretation of the humanities and of history, and civil laws themselves. As a consequence, many people are shaken" (*PC*, art. 7).

(3) One of the most important elements for a theological consideration of atheism is that it is no longer approached schematically, or offhandedly, but in a differentiated manner. This differentiation begins with the question: What precisely do we mean by atheism? What does a person mean when he says he is an atheist, or professes atheism? We no longer have ready-made answers to these questions, but attend to the situation openly and unpretentiously: "The word 'atheism' is applied to phenomena which are quite distinct from one another. For while God is expressly denied by some, others believe that man can assert absolutely nothing about him. Still others use such a method so to scrutinize the question of God as to make it seem devoid of meaning. Many, unduly transgressing the limits of the positive sciences, contend that everything can be explained by this kind of scientific reasoning alone, or, by contrast, they altogether disallow that there is any absolute truth. Some laud man so extravagantly that their faith in God lapses into a kind of anemia, though they seem more inclined to affirm man than to deny God. Again some form for themselves such a fallacious idea of God that when they repudiate this figment they are by no means rejecting the God of the gospel. Some never get to the point of raising questions about God, since they seem to

experience no religious stirrings, nor do they see why they should trouble themselves about religion" (*PC*, art. 19).

Interpretation of this important point should take into account the variety of possibility, form, and motivation in atheism. We shall now consider these aspects briefly against the horizon of theological reflection.

What is denied in atheism? That God could not exist or is not real? (What do we mean by "real"?) Or that it is impossible to know God, to say anything about him positively, or categorically, on the basis of the particular premisses of the various sciences?

The numerous questions implied in atheism specify a possible answer.

When it is said that nothing positive can be said about God, that can mean a pure and radical negation. However, is it not also the case that every theology recognizes that statements about God stand under the sign of negation—that what we know about God more properly signifies what God is not than articulates what God is? Does not the mystic speak of the fact that God is "a pure nothing"? What he means is simply that statements cannot get hold of what is "beyond" all the categorical determinations of the world of experience ("beyond" not in the sense of spatial distance, but in the sense of the comprehensive and all-embracing ground transcending all being). If God is not a being among other beings, an object among objects, if he is not the first member of a causal series, but the transcendental ground of whatever is, then the categories and concepts which serve for the knowledge of being find their limit with the knowledge of God. This latter sort of knowledge must be satisfied with the determination of "not" and "not so," by describing God as "in-finite" and "un-created." That does not exclude the fact that these negative determinations imply positive statements, such as that the infinite is the ground of the finite, or that the uncreated is the ground of creation.

It must also be said that there is a legitimate methodological, scientific atheism, because God cannot be confronted or known within the possibilities and methods of the experiential and natural sciences. Thus Laplace was correct when he declared that he did not require the hypothesis of God in his researches. God is no substitute for an understanding of the world.

In the previous chapter we noted that the distinction between God and world, creator and creation, as contained in the Christian faith, along with the de-divinization of the world as a finite, godless world, formed the premiss for natural science and technology, which have established the independence of the world and are in the service of mankind. God does not appear in the world of natural science. He cannot be demonstrated on the basis of the world, but on the same basis neither can he be denied. Natural science and technology are not possible in a mythical world-view where cosmogony becomes theogony, where concrete and empirical causes are not recognized, where only divine powers and causalities are accepted. If, further, the concept "reality" is derived from experience and restricted to it, then it must be said that God, in fact, is not real—in the sense of this understanding of reality. "The God who is, is not."[2]

The position that it is impossible to know God perhaps implies only a specific mode of knowledge that does not exclude other possibilities whereby man can know God, for example through practical reason, or the existential confirmation of transcendence, as formulated by Karl Jaspers with his usual terseness: "no existence without transcendence."

Whoever denies a knowledge of God on the basis of a specific and perhaps restricted conception of knowledge does not thereby deny God, or become an atheist (a fate that Kant has suffered under for so long; who, because of his critique of the proof of God, has often been called an "all-destroyer").

Atheism, as it has been presented so far, can draw attention to something that must ever be considered anew by theology—the mystery of divine being (which is not a created being); the uniqueness of the knowledge of God; and the obscurity of the thought that must attend such knowledge, a thought that must humble itself and recognize that what it does not know goes far

[2] W. Kasper, "Unsere Gottesbeziehung angesichts der sich wandelnden Gottesvorstellung," in *Catholica* 20 (1966), p. 261. The formulation itself goes back to D. Bonhoeffer.

beyond what it does know, a thought that is aware of its limits and accepts its statements as approximations. Understood in this manner, atheism can have a purifying and clarifying function, as indeed it has had in various religions and in the history of religion. Joseph Ratzinger puts it this way: "Atheism is not necessarily the denial of the absolute as such, but its transfer to pure formlessness; that is, it is a protest against the form with which the absolute is identified. That is precisely the great and irreplaceable role of atheism in the history of religion. The formation of the divine, in fact, ultimately leads to the humanization of God, and thus to the absolutization of humanity in terms of very specific attitudes towards and interpretations of man. We find here not only the essence, but the 'non-essence,' of religion, so that religion becomes not only the great prospect of, but the great danger to mankind. Because we are dealing here with the absolute, the humanization and concretization of the absolute can lead to the most dreadful consequences, whereby the group, the system, the establishment posit themselves absolutely, and posit everything that opposes them outside the confines of humanity as pure evil. Because the very nature of man makes it so that every formation leads to the separation, and thus to the false humanization, of God, every formation must be accompanied by the great counter-movement of purification, which attends to the continual supersedure of form, and ultimately to the deification of God. A Christian cannot simply regard the positive formations of religions in the history of the world as good, and the atheistic frame of mind as pure sinfulness, but rather must view both attitudes—formation and purification—as mutually fulfilling and delineated by the process of rise and fall."[3]

Such assertions, of course, must not force the conclusion that atheism can be evaluated simply in such a positive manner. They are intended to show that such an interpretation is possible and legitimate, and that it is to be pursued with intensive and wide-

[3] "Atheismus," in *Wahrheit und Zeugnis*, edited by M. Schmaus and A. Läpple (Dusseldorf, 1964), p. 96.

ranging receptiveness before a global denial and rejection of atheism is pronounced.

What is denied in atheism? In the Council's pastoral constitution, it is pointed out that many atheists first construct an image of God and then struggle against it and deny it, and that they thereby presume to have rejected God as such, or the God of Christian revelation, although—such is the opinion of the Council—this God is not at all the God of the gospel (article 19).

This point raises again a problem that has already been considered, namely, that man must not, as the Old Testament demands, "carve an idol or make some other likeness" of God (Exodus 20, 4), but listen to God through faith in the *word*. Otherwise, man becomes capable of thinking and speaking of God only through an image and a likeness. Then it becomes forgotten that every image and form falls short of the greater mystery of God. Thus we are given the constant task of moving from the reality of the image to what is intended by, and different from, the image, of not identifying God, whom we cannot express without an image and a likeness, with any image and likeness.

We should also keep in mind that imaged representations of God change and pass away in the course of human life. Many who deny God deny perhaps only a naïve representation of God which one cannot accept intellectually, a representation that has not kept pace with the rest of one's knowledge and deeper experiences. One denies the God of picture books and childish songs.

If God for many men functions as the stand-in for causes that have not as yet been discovered, as the unknown X that is introduced when immanent explanations cannot yet be given, then it follows that a God so understood begins to fade away as causes are discovered for which he had temporarily been the explanation. Such a God dies the death of constant diminishment. However, a declaration of the death of this God is not atheism. Theology, though, must clarify the situation by showing that the affirmation of God as the lord and creator of the world does not coincide with the supposition of God as a working hypothesis for the purpose of explaining the world.

How often God is made into the projection of human wishes, fears, and needs! How often the name of God is misused in order to escape true responsibility, for the sake of human indolence and passivity, as an alibi for flight from the difficulties of life!

It also cannot be denied that God has been put forward as the guarantor of numerous situations and ideologies, such as the God who "always accompanies the strongest army," the "God whose strength lies in force," the God who must declare the goals of power politics as the will and act of divine providence. The characterization of the kingdom of God as offering to the poor and neglected in this vale of tears the compensation and consolation of the beyond is sufficient grounds for the Marxist qualification of religion as the "opium of the people," which hinders the liberation of man from his self-alienation and enslavement and from unjust social and economic conditions. That God had been made into a description of the world of psychic unconsciousness led Sigmund Freud to label religion an illusion.

The denial and rejection of God, understood and represented in such a manner, is not atheism, but the destruction of idols and a service to belief in God. Atheism, if pursued and formulated in this manner, becomes a test and purification of religion. It ascertains the yearning and "passion" for an ever greater God and protests against "all caricatures of the infinite, which constitute an offense against the spirit par excellence."[4] When Dietrich Bonhoeffer postulates, on the basis of these premisses, a "religionless Christianity," we can do nothing but agree to it. In parentheses, however, it must be said that Bonhoeffer's conception of religion has to do not with the essence, but with the non-essence, of religion; a non-essence, nonetheless, for which many religious men, and many Christians, are responsible.[5] Paul

[4] R. Garaudy, "Wertung der Religion in Marxismus," in *Christentum und Marxismus heute* (Vienna-Frankfurt-Zürich, 1966), p. 84.

[5] Cf. H. Fries, "Die Botschaft von Christus in einer Welt ohne Gott," in *Wir und die andern*, pp. 273–314.

Ricoeur typifies the immediate consequences of this situation in light of Freud's proclaimed atheism: "We have attained a sufficient distance to have absorbed the truth of Freud's position with respect to religion. Freud has strengthened the faith of the unbeliever, but has scarcely begun to purify the faith of the believer."[6] The Council indulged in no illusions with regard to this state of affairs: "For, taken as a whole, atheism is not a spontaneous development but stems from a variety of causes, including a critical reaction against religious beliefs, and in some places against the Christian religion in particular. Hence believers can have more than a little to do with the birth of atheism. To the extent that they neglect their own training in the faith, or teach erroneous doctrine, or are deficient in their religious, moral, or social life, they must be said to conceal rather than reveal the authentic face of God and religion" (article 19).

The Council text draws attention to the possibility of atheism as a protest against evil in the world. Such an atheism is basically a "concerned and combative atheism." It is, as Karl Rahner has put it, a question hidden in an answer. This question concerns the absence, hiddenness, silence, and impotence of God. The question: Where is God? or: Where, God, do we find you?—in light of the suffering, the suffering of the guiltless, in the world; in light of the triumph of violence and injustice; in light of the impenetrability of so many circumstances and experiences—becomes the conviction: There is no God. This atheistic "anxiety" hidden in questions is a theme found throughout the Bible, beginning with the complaints and lamentations put forth in the Book of Job and in numerous psalms, and even in the cry of Christ crucified: "My God, why hast thou forsaken me?" (Matthew 27: 46). The passion and crucifixion of Christ are the most moving signs of this question and the situation it represents.

The idea of a hidden God, the *theologia crucis*, as proclaimed by Martin Luther, is a fundamental aspect of the Christian faith. It is both a test and a temptation that it will always have to face.

[6] P. Ricoeur, "Atheism of Freudian Psychoanalysis," in *Concilium* (Glen Rock: 2 (1966), p. 435; London: 6, 2, p. 31).

The *theologia crucis* seeks to give expression to the fact that God is different, that he acts and operates in a manner entirely different from human and religious representations of God—as in the *theologia gloriae* of the God of love, the God "who can create whatever he desires."[7]

The cross of Jesus Christ can, in light of the suffering in the world, lead to the denial of a God which man has made according to his own likeness and image, a God which he can control insofar as he seeks to determine what God can or cannot do, what he can or cannot allow. But it cannot lead to the denial of the God of which the New Testament speaks and bears witness.

If by atheism we mean the fact that belief in God does not signify some sort of life force in human existence, that the plans, understandings, and decisions of man must be pursued *etsi non daretur Deus*; if God, in fact, is characterized by his absence and silence; then not only should the believer turn to matters of disbelief and pursue them with the etiquette of practical atheism—he must. For the priorities of his own life are determined by these same principles and laws. In other words, belief always implies disbelief. The *simul* of *fidelis et infidelis* is a fact. Faith is accompanied by non-faith, credibility by incredibility.[8] We find disbelief and godlessness within our own selves. In a variation of the well-known phrase, we might say that just as there are anonymous Christians among non-Christians, so there are anonymous atheists among Christians. This situation holds not merely because the Christian does not open his life enough to the word, the promise, and the authority of faith, or because he is lax, forgetful, or careless, but because faith itself is always a risk. It is not a self-establishing or incontestable possession. As the total act of the selfhood and freedom

[7] Cf. H. Fries, "Die Grundanliegen der Theologie Luthers in der Sicht der katholischen Theologie der Gegenwart," in *Wir und die andern*, p. 163f.

[8] J. B. Metz "Unbelief and a Theological Problem," in *Concilium* (Glen Rock: 1 [1965], p. 487; London: 7, 1, p. 32); cf. in a different connection, R. Bultmann, "Das Problem der natürlichen Theologie," in *Glauben und Verstehen I*, pp. 294–312, particularly pp. 298, 311f.

of man, faith must be constantly renewed. It must prevail against the overpowering strength of the complexity and confusions of experience, as the completely other, as the "nevertheless," as the unobservable that is grounded in word, promise, and witness. The believer well knows that he must conduct himself with fear and trembling. The passage from the gospel: "Lord, I do believe; help my unbelief" (Mark 9: 23), is not mere fine rhetoric, nor a hypocritical understatement, but a deep acknowledgement of truth.

We have attempted to introduce some theological reflections concerning the phenomenon of atheism in a way that gets behind mere words and seeks out a differentiation of the various forms and motives of atheism. This approach specifies the challenges and critical questions posed by atheism to faith for the consideration of theology. As a consequence, we have come to see that the negativity previously addressed to an improperly understood atheism—the *damnamus* or *anathema sit*—is not at all sufficient. At the same time, we have formed the premisses for those questions that still remain and for those tasks that still stand before theology with regard to atheism.

III

We cannot expect an exhaustive treatment of this topic, any more than we could with the topics that preceded it. The best we can do is offer a few hints and suggest some points of view. The pastoral constitution declares that, irrespective of the rejection and condemnation of atheism legitimately expressed in past and present times "out of loyalty to God and mankind," it is a fact that the Church "strives to detect in the atheistic mind the hidden causes for the denial of God. Conscious of how weighty are the questions which atheism raises, and motivated by love for all men, she believes these questions ought to be examined more seriously and more profoundly" (article 21). The situation presented here clearly suggests the need for a review.

We immediately come upon a word in this context that was a basic term during the Council, and has since almost become a household word—*dialogue*. The theologians of the Church should enter into dialogue with atheists and with all non-believers. This dialogue is demanded not only in view of the many concrete tasks and practical goals which require the cooperation of all men for the construction of a human world, the true structure of the world—it is demanded as a *theological task*.

Such a dialogue must take place today in the area of anthropology. Today it is man, not nature or the cosmos, who is the immediate and necessary theme of dialogue—man, the creature of opportunity and promise. The reason for this is that atheism has been proposed in the name of freedom and justice for mankind, in the name of rooting out self-alienation; further, because humanism has become the goal of modern atheism, particularly as it has been influenced by Marxism.[9]

We have already cited the pastoral constitution to show that it is much more interested in an affirmation of man than in a denial of God. This attitude is strengthened in the following passage: "Modern atheism often takes on a systematic expression, which, in addition to other arguments against God, stretches the desire for human independence to such a point that it finds difficulties with any kind of dependence on God. Those who profess atheism of this sort maintain that it gives man freedom to be an end unto himself, the sole artisan and creator of his own history. They claim that this freedom cannot be reconciled with the affirmation of a Lord who is author and purpose of all things, or at least that this freedom makes such an affirmation altogether superfluous. The sense of power which modern technical progress generates in man can give color to such a doctrine.

"Not to be overlooked among the forms of modern atheism is that which anticipates the liberation of man especially through

[9] Cf. John Courtney Murray, *The Problem of God: Yesterday and Today* (New Haven, 1964); A. Schaff, *Marxismus und das menschliche Individuum* (Vienna–Frankfurt–Zürich, 1965); *Marxistisches und christliches Weltverständnis* (Vienna-Freiburg, 1966); *Christentum und Marxismus heute* (Vienna–Frankfurt–Zürich, 1966); and especially, R. Garaudy, *Wertung der Religion im Marxismus*, pp. 77–98.

his economic and social emancipation. This form argues that by its nature religion thwarts such liberation by arousing man's hope for a deceptive future life, thereby diverting him from the constructing of the earthly city. Consequently, when the proponents of this doctrine gain governmental power they vigorously fight against religion. They promote atheism by using those means of pressure which public power has at its disposal. Such is especially the case in the work of educating the young" (article 20).

These words bring to the fore that fundamental attitude which never ceases to contend that God must die in order that man may live; that if God exists, man cannot truly be man. "The will to be an atheist is the will to be a man; and to be a man means to strive to be like God."[10]

Atheism, therefore, is a *movement towards the liberation* of man from man *for man*—for his happiness, his authenticity, for a human and humanized world—the inspiration not only to understand the world, but to change it. Atheism is the liberation from religious control, from restrictions placed upon reason. Atheism moves away from an alien ethics of legalism, an ethics declared by the command and will of God, to a human, autonomous ethics, a morals without sin. Such an attitude envisions a "holiness without God" (Albert Camus). The ethical wholly constitutes itself and is in need of no ultimate completion or grand display.

For the post-Christian and post-theistic man, Christianity, as well as religion and belief in God, are things of the past, upon which he can look back without anger—for he is a man who feels himself moved to live and exist in the new fundamental of spontaneous self-understanding.

It is precisely at this crucial point, in the question *concerning man*, that is, concerning his determination, his origin, his nature, his goal, that theology enters the fray. This is the point at which a dialogue can begin.

A few notes of clarification are in order. Theology is directly

[10] John Courtney Murray, *The Problem of God: Yesterday and Today.*

aware of the fact that atheism possesses an eminently anthropological and theological component: namely, because man is the image and likeness of God, he can project God according to this image and come to understand God as his counter-image, such that it can truly be said that "the God in man struggles against and overwhelms the God above and beyond man, because there seems to be no room left for the higher God in terms of human demands. But in this striving, man has fallen prey to the revenge of finitude, from which he can never escape even though he perpetually seeks a means of escape."[11]

Furthermore, theology—following the advice of the Council: "The atheist should be simply invited to assess in freedom the gospel of Jesus Christ" (article 21)—must draw attention to the fact, by a comparison of theories, that no philosophy has made such great, such true, and such humanly verifiable statements about the life and death of man, and about the history and community of human existence, as the Christian faith; or in other words, that *anthropocentrism is not the contrary to theocentrism,* but its legitimate fruit.[12]

Theology must make clear that the acceptance and affirmation of God is not a prejudice or a concurrence, but the possibility of fundamental, transcendental freedom for man. God is not another co-efficient hindering the work of freedom. God is the validating ground of the freedom of the being and nature of man. God stands to all beings in an utterly incomparable relationship, that is, he makes possible the actual uniqueness of the reality of the created order. For man, as a person, that signifies reason and freedom.[13]

Theology must make clear that man, if he properly understands himself, is constantly going beyond himself. Human

[11] B. Welte, "Die philosophische Gotteserkenntnis und die Möglichkeit des Atheismus," in *Concilium* 2, p. 406, and "Nietzsches Atheismus und das Christentum," in *Auf der Spur des Ewigen* (Freiburg-Basel-Vienna, 1965), pp. 228–261, particularly p. 245; F. Ulrich, *Atheismus und Menschwerdung* (Einsiedeln, 1966).

[12] J. B. Metz, *Christian Anthropocentricism*; Harvey Cox, *The Secular City.*

[13] Cf. J. B. Metz, "Freiheit," in *HthG* I, pp. 403–414, and "Freiheit als philosophisch-theologisches Grenzproblem," in *Gott in Welt* I, pp. 287–314.

existence does not ground itself, but rather recognizes its indebtedness to the co-affirmation of the unconditioned (which is not directly accessible to man in the world as such) in the fundamental acts of his spirit—in his questions, his knowledge, his life, his responsibility for the decisions of his conscience.[14] Without the unconditioned confronting him unconditionally, man can neither understand nor properly realize himself. Theology must explain and interpret those statements that are essential to existential theology, for to speak of God means to speak of man; to speak of man means to speak of God.[15]

We are thereby led to ask whether man, understood in this manner, is alienated from himself through the acceptance, or rather through the rejection, of God? It should also be noted that the values which are lived by man today and explicitly affirmed by atheism—purity, selflessness, solidarity, community, brotherhood, hope—have their true source and deepest foundation in Christian belief in God. Can we expect a perpetuation of the permanent validity of such values if they are cut off at their root? Theology is bound to pose the alternatives: *humanism without God* or *humanism with God*? It need not fear this concurrence, nor need it be apprehensive of verification through the totality of human experience. In the fundamental and comprehensive testimony of the Christian faith in the incarnation of God can be found the ultimate meaning of humanism and the legitimate understanding of anthropocentrism.

The statements that introduce the theme of atheism in the Council's pastoral constitution speak of the unique value of man found in his call to union with God. "Man is called to a dialogue with God by his very nature, for he exists only because he has been created and sustained in love by God. And he does not live in the full measure of truth if he does not accept this love freely and return it to his creator" (article 19). That means, in line with our anthropological analyses, that atheism is not something

[14] K. Rahner has done the most important work in these areas.

[15] R. Bultmann, "Welchen Sinn hat es, von Gott zu reden?," in *Glauben und Verstehen* I, pp. 26–37, and "Das Gottesgedanke und der moderne Mensch," in *Glauben und Verstehen* IV, pp. 113–127; cf. also G. Ebeling, *Word and Faith*.

fundamental; it is something secondary, a reaction. Man does not enter into the world as an atheist. Thus Gerhard Szczesny's position, that atheism *precedes* theism, in inadmissible. Other similar positions are no less admissible: "I did not come upon the idea of a personal God by myself. Thus there is nothing to prevent me from disregarding it. Only the Christians trouble me with this question, but they do not say how it is possible to bring God into experience. The lectures in a book which try to reproduce the experience of others do not constitute my experience."

In response it must be said that we are not dealing with experiences from literature, but with an experience that is possible for every man who is not satisfied with the mere determination of facts or the manipulation of exactitudes, but who is concerned about questions concerning the ground, the meaning, the origin, and the future of man.[16]

These thoughts bridge over to a further consideration with respect to atheism, namely, the question of "culpable" and "non-culpable" atheism. The Second Vatican Council, it should be noted, restrained itself on this question (in distinction from earlier ecclesiastical declarations in which atheism was attended with guilt). Karl Rahner has made some important observations in this connection.[17] The basic thesis is: If a man declares himself an atheist in good conscience, fulfilling the requirements of his moral consciousness, seeking the truth for truth's sake, doing good for good's sake, if he loves selflessly, then he not only has an implicit knowledge of God as the one who "confronts" man "unconditionally," he affirms this God in freedom and in action as the ground—the God both hidden and yet known, the ultimate premiss and authority of human action. Thus there can be an atheism which fulfills and realizes existentially this transcendental experience of God, but yet does not articulate and interpret this relation, since it has no adequate, that is, objective,

[16] Cf. H. Fries, *Ärgernis und Widerspruch: Christentum und Kirche im Spiegel gegenwärtiger Kritik* (Würzburg, 1965), pp. 32–41.

[17] K. Rahner, "Atheism," in *Sacramentum Mundi* I (London and New York, 1968); on the question itself, cf. M. Seckler, *Instinkt und Glaubenswille nach Thomas von Aquin* (Main, 1961), particularly pp. 232–258.

concept of God. There is, then, the possibility that, at the level of categorial reflection, atheism can co-exist in the same subject "with a transcendental theism affirmed in freedom."

This is an entirely different sort of atheism from that which not only does not interpret the transcendental relation to God correctly, but denies it in a conscious act of freedom, and suppresses it in a culpable act of disloyalty against true conscience. Here there is an ultimate "no" to the very fundamental relation of man to God. When we speak of a non-culpable atheism, we mean a categorial atheism, at the level of linguistic and conceptual objectivation. Culpable atheism is always a lived, transcendental atheism, which repudiates the very heart of man.

IV

These theological reflections must not be concluded without at least a brief attempt at a specific, theological answer to contemporary atheism.

Christian anthropocentrism—to speak of God means to speak of man—the fundamental Christian command to love one's neighbor, Christian brotherhood, the identification of Jesus Christ with "the least of his brethren" (Matthew 25: 40, 45), these are the impulses and the principles of a theology which takes Christianity as a radical humanism, and which makes God into a functional concept of humanity and the community of man.[18] Christianity distinguishes itself from other forms of humanism only in terms of its premisses, not in terms of its content. Jesus Christ is the exemplary realization of that relation which establishes true humanism—for he is a man for others. The fundamental theme of his message is service, receptivity, love, solidarity, community. As a result: "Anthropology is the constant; Christology is the variable."[19]

[18] H. Braun, "Die Problematic einer Theologie des Neuen Testaments," in *Gesammelte Studien zum Neuen Testament und seiner Umwelt* (Tübingen, 1962), p. 334f.

[19] H. Braun, "Der Sinn der neutestamentlichen Christologie," in *Zeitschrift für Theologie und Kirche* 54 (1957), p. 368.

In line with the message of Christianity, properly understood, it is the intra-human (or better, inter-human), horizontal dimension alone that is important. The Anglican bishop John A. T. Robinson, the most influential proponent of this theological dimension, formulates this view in the simple phrase: nothing is prescribed except love.[20] As a consequence, we hear of a theological "Robinsonism," which, in carrying out the imagery, attaches insufficient value to the vertical, or God-man, relation, insofar as it attempts to integrate it totally into the horizontal relations. This is a quest, or yearning, for a *theology without God*. Such a theology alone, it is argued, is in a position to dialogue with atheism, because it alone can conduct such a dialogue without resorting to mediating devices that supposedly adhere to an outdated world-view. Robinson formulates and affirms this situation explicitly with the question: "Can a sincere contemporary individual be anything but an atheist?"[21]

From a theological point of view, it must be said that the exclusion of the vertical union of God with man, the reduction of the Christian to the human (this is so-called Christological humanism), undermines the very essence of Christianity. It is a new variant of the persistent attempt to modernize Christianity by doing away with its distinctiveness. The highly commendable effort to find a horizon of understanding, and a point of contact, for the preaching of the Christian message runs the danger of making this message optional.

Without the God-man dimension, neither the mystery of the person and life of Christ, nor the meaning of Christian faith and existence, can be determined. In terms of imagery again, without the vertical, the horizontal cannot be maintained. The horizontalization of Christianity involves its reduction to the limits, projects, determinations, and requirements of man. It signifies an approach to the Christian faith according to the manipulation of man. To speak yet of Christianity is a mere matter of convention and tradition. For Christianity has nothing

[20] *Gott ist anders*, p. 121.

[21] *A New Reformation?* (Westminster, 1965). For a response to Robinson, cf. H. Fries, *Ärgernis und Widerspruch*, pp. 101–121.

to say and to promise but what is already possible. It is a very significant fact, a sort of "test case" for this theology, that prayer no longer has its proper place of value, but rather is replaced by meditation on humanity.

Leo Scheffczyk has justly remarked, "A religion which has nothing *more* to say than what is of use to man, perhaps only saying it a bit differently, will soon have *nothing* more to say to man. A Church which involved itself exclusively in service to man and to the world would set for itself a role similar to that allowed in the Marxist doctrine of the state; that is, it slowly loses its significance and ultimately negates itself. The risk of such self-dissolution of faith into an inner-worldly religiosity can be endured only if the Church derives its service to man from its service to God, and devotes itself totally to the latter."[22] Nothing is thereby taken away from service to man in the world. On the contrary, it merely specifies its ultimate ground, namely, God in Christ and Christ in man, the Christ who makes service of love possible, who bestows the worthiness to be loved upon all men. Without this vertical love of God, the love of man, both in everyday situations and in its special forms—love of enemies and those who are unsympathetic, love of the poor, the sick, and the feeble, love as forgiveness and reconciliation—would be unintelligible, unrealistic, and impossible.

The full meaning of this truth appears in the "Our Father." The vertical, which is expressed in the prayer to the "Father," makes possible the "our." Without truly personal inter-subjectivity between God and man, the real depth and ultimate relation of the "community of man," being human for others, would be lost. Thus it can truly be said, "Whoever has not known the countenance of God in contemplation, will not recognize it in action, even if it should present itself on the countenance of poverty and suffering."[23]

[22] L. Scheffczyk, "Kirche im Wandel," in *Wort und Wahrheit* 21 (1966), p. 752. Also, H. Gollwitzer, in H. W. Augustin, *Diskussion zu Bischof Robinsons Gott ist anders* (Munich, 1964), p. 122. On the problem of the functionalization of the concept of God, cf. H. Gollwitzer, *Die Existenz Gottes im Bekenntnis des Glaubens* (Munich, 1963).

[23] H. Urs von Balthasar, *Love Alone*. In a number of works this theologian has opposed the reduction of Christianity to humanism.

Yet another tendency in theology—one which seems more provocative as a defining concept of Christianity than the humanism we have just discussed—appears to be an even more compatible partner in dialogue with atheism. We refer to "God is dead" theology, theology in a post-theistic epoch. Among the representatives of this theology in America are the W. Hamilton, P. van Buren, and Thomas J. J. Altizer. In Germany its best-known proponent is Dorothee Sölle.[24]

Different elements and aspects are here fused together and radicalized in this theology: thus Robinson's idea, as set forth in *Honest to God*, that "We must do away with our notions of God," while at the same time we are called upon to acknowledge the silence and absence of God, the phenomenon of the secularized world come of age, as represented by Dietrich Bonhoeffer in his *kenosis* theology, or theology of the cross, together with the conception of a religionless Christianity.

God is dead theology begins with the phenomenon of a world without God, that is, with the contemporary period being regarded as the post-theistic epoch. This epoch is characterized by the death of God. The true experience of the death of God, however, allows neither for the theist, "for whom there is a God," nor for the atheist, for whom God does not exist. This is the experience of men for whom God has died, and who are concerned about this death.

Dorothee Sölle (whose ideas form the basis of the following discussion) builds her theological and Christological position upon these considerations. She fastens upon the concept of "representation," which for her has a double-edged meaning. To represent means to answer for someone at a certain time and under certain conditions, to take his place, during which "the one for whom the substitution is made appears not to be present, or dead." Thus representation is not a temporary, but a long-lasting and binding affair. As distinct from substitution, which suggests exchangeability, representation implies the irreplaceability of the person. Man is irreplaceable, but representable.

[24] D. Sölle, *The Representative* (London, 1967).

Within the limits of temporality, representation involves the total relatedness of mankind. As a consequence, we have as a fundamental thesis: Christ represents us before God and he represents God to man.

Christ believes and hopes, acts and suffers, "on our behalf," in our place, not in order to dispense us from something, but in order to instruct us. Thus he shows himself to be the true teacher.

On the cross, Christ identified himself with all men, whom God had forsaken. The forsakenness of God is a lasting situation for man, and cannot be eliminated by any sort of "exaltation." Christ is the representative of those men who still put up with God, who, with him, still wait for the coming of God. Christ opens himself to the forsakenness of God. He assumes a *kenosis* for which we ourselves are not capable. He does this so that we too can do it. Christ dies for us so that we ourselves can learn how to die.

This very same Christ is also the representative of *God*. Dorothee Sölle is very explicit: he is not a substitute for a dead God, but the representative of the living, but absent, God. Christ holds a place open for the absent God. He frees the future for him. He is not the final revealer, but the precursor of God burdened with "provisionality." Thus Christ is he who plays the role of God in the world, but he plays God in the "conditions of weakness." Easter is not the ultimate victory, but an anticipated hope, a "category of meaning" in the "shadow of the cross."

The way in which man, who lives in the realization of the death of God and waits for the return of God, can open and deliver himself to God, is not by waiting for the hereafter, or striving for happiness, or by believing in the objectivations of God in "miracles, acts of providence, or the history of revelation," but through the deliverance of man to man. There is no other (direct) surrender to God. God has communicated himself to the world. God is to be found in the other. Love neither seeks nor needs a heaven. "Love is the representation of the silent God in the world."

The theological answer to this extreme and provocative position must take the form of indirect theological ecumenism, for it is a problem which today is directed at the whole of theology.

Very generally it can be said that this theology, in its clearly recognizable tendency to humanism and a radically horizontal immanentism, is not so much a problem in terms of what it says (the idea of representation is a universal principle of the history of salvation, and a key concept for Christology, ecclesiology, and theological anthropology,[25] although it does not lead to those results which Sölle believes are thereby drawn) as in what it *does not say* in order to remain in style and maintain its contacts for dialogue.

Such "negativity" has to do with its fundamental position. It is a legitimate and necessary task to bring Christianity into a correlation with humanity, yet we must ask whether, in light of the narrow anthropological position that is represented here, the anticipated analyses and the questions derived from them have not already determined the possible answers and contents of faith. The question stipulates "that the gospel must obey. Thus God can no longer be viewed as the one who supplies the needs that are clearly found in man. It must be decided on human terms alone, exclusive of the gospel, what sort of assistance man needs."[26] This attitude overlooks the fact that faith itself is the cause of certain questions.

A further point has to do with Christology. Dorothee Sölle insists upon the "not yet" of the coming of Christ and interprets finality in an inadmissible manner: "Whoever has the final Christ needs no future." As a consequence, too little consideration is given to the distinction between the Old and New Testaments, the Christ event is reduced to Good Friday, and attention is given too exclusively to the impotence and God-forsakenness of Christ on the cross. That is only *one* side of the New Testament witness. There is also the insurpassable message of the *oneness* of Jesus with the Father, especially in the passion, the

[25] Cf. J. Ratzinger, "Stellvertretung," in *HthG* II, pp. 56–575.

[26] Cf. H. Gollwitzer, *Von der Stellvertretung Gottes* (Munich, 1967), p. 29.

central witness of the exaltation manifest in the resurrection of Christ from the dead, the coming fulfillment of the victory of God, the initiation of a new life and hope for man. This is the fundamental witness of Jesus as the Christ and the Lord. This message cannot be translated into the words: Christ is "a precursor, an advocate, an actor."

God is dead theology, concerned as it is about the connection between the present and the future, is simply unable to cope with the deeper connection that holds in the mystery of the person and destiny of Christ.

In this way, the "distinction of being Christian" is lost. It is quite difficult to see how such a theology can adopt a specific, rather than a mere conventional, orientation to Jesus Christ, such that the person and destiny of Christ do not become an arbitrary symbol or metaphor. It is even more difficult to understand how Jesus Christ is the representative of God and man, how all later action and suffering are anticipated in Christ. Such a claim, which is at the same time a universal promise, is only possible through the sort of trans-limitation of space and time that is present in the resurrection of Jesus from the dead and in the truth of the exalted Christ.

Only because Jesus, in a manner known only to him, is the Son of God, can he intercede to him on our behalf. Because he is resurrected, he can be with us until the end of the world and identify with each one of us. Because God becomes identified with him, he is, for all men and for all times, the fulfillment of the promises that are given in the word of God. It is precisely in this sense that Jesus Christ is the Representative.

If, to carry these thoughts further, God is only a name for the achievement of love between men, a symbol of the community of mankind, then what can be said to a man who is forsaken by all men and devoid of all love? And who can deny that there are such men, in countless number, and today more than at any other time in history?

We can close these reflections with a quotation from Helmut Gollwitzer's discussion with Dorothee Sölle: "Dorothee Sölle has written, 'It has become impossible to accept naïve theism, a direct, childlike relation to the Father above the stars in heaven,' and she has gone on to explain in another place, 'I do not know how, after Auschwitz, it is possible to praise God, who directs everything so magnificently,' and again, 'There is no way back to the Father of children, who directs the course and paths of the wind and clouds.' What can be said to all of this? Anyone who has not closed his eyes entirely knows that traditional language about trust in God, the Father in heaven, can be the meanest excuse, the most cold-hearted dismissal, sounding like scorn in the ears of those who are afflicted, and that the laughter of scorn that greets such words can be that of Job. But these words themselves? Have they lost their truth through misuse? Have they lost their truth in the past and present horror of this century? In what sense is there 'no way back' to them? If they are not true today, they were also not true earlier, even during the horror of the Thirty Years War, since they conflict no less with that event than they do with the horror of Auschwitz, Hiroshima, and Vietnam. Was the request to trust in the promise, 'I will always be with you,' any less important then than today, amidst the horror, the senseless circumstances, the exposure to the inhumanity of those in power, within a world without God? Was trust in God more of a possibility then than today? What turns me against such statements, I must confess, is the devaluation and disrespect they contain, as if the attitudes of previous centuries, and language about the direction and control exercised by God the Father, owed their sole existence to thoughtlessness and naïve optimism. They are offered *in extremis*, in open opposition. They recognize the Job situation, they speak of the God-forsakenness on Golgotha and read into it the Easter response, the promise, 'I am there.' What they say is not the expression of their own observation, the result of an optimistic knowledge of life. Even when these men express their prayer and witness as a statement of their own conviction and experience, what they say is not from themselves, but to themselves. In the darkness of torment, they hold the light of promise before themselves and call out the words of promise in trust and consolation. And they have, in this manner, thought much more than nothing—and certainly no less than when we interpret these simple, childlike words. They were for them as little 'self-evident' as they are for us. Whoever is of the opinion that 'we today' can no longer pray in such a way implies that in the past the horrors of the world were experienced less, regarded as if by unsuspecting children, and that the hope of those who lived then was an illusion, able to maintain itself only within certain limits, or that the Fatherhood of God is a claim which holds on sunny days, and easily believed by those with the heart of a child, but shattered now by the burdens of this century. Such a person minimizes the burdens of earlier times in order to demonstrate the impossibility of prayer for our times, and regards the promise as a limited one, valid only once, on the cross, but not during the night of the cross. Insofar as belief in the acceptance of the present-day Fatherhood of God is declared to be impossible for our times, the supposition is that it is regarded as a possibility for the men of earlier times.

"The Christian faith is fundamentally set against this position, for faith is not a human possibility. The God of Christian faith is not a possible God who is understood as the result of possible human modes of observation. The fact that he directs everything in majesty cannot be determined by observation of events in the world. Trust in him is not a mode of relation possible for people who know nothing of evil days—of gas chambers, napalm, and nuclear war. He, whose promise was given to us in the preaching of the Bible, is an impossible God. To know, to love, and to call to him was then, as it is now, 'impossible through the power of reason alone,' but possible through the power of the word of promise itself, which flies flush in the face of appearance and stands in contradiction to appearance—through the spirit of this Word, the Holy Spirit.

"The result is a complete relativization of the distinctions of time. What is impossible today was also yesterday; what was possible yesterday, is so today also."[27]

[27] *Ibid.*, pp. 142–144.

There is nothing to add to these words. Christian faith stands firm against this challenge too. It is neither confounded nor contradicted. It has been led into its most difficult temptation, which is also the hour and the place of its greatest confirmation.

Index of Names